THE W IN HER EYE

POEMS · BY WOMEN

EDITOR · RACHEL · LEVER

INTRODUCED BY
LIZ LOCHHEAD

ILLUSTRATIONS · BY
JOSEPHINE McCORMICK

PYRAMID
PRESS

Pyramid
Poetry Press
is the imprint of
Hen House Publications
Hawerby Hall
North Thoresby
Lincs DN36 5QL

Printed by Redwood Books
Trowbridge, Wiltshire

First Printed In The UK
In 1995

ISBN 1 899981 00 4

British Library Cataloguing in Publication Data.
A catalogue record of this book is available from the British Library

INTRODUCTION

WHEN we read poetry we experience emotions. Pure, sharp, distinct, plural, contradictory, but summoned instantly by the sensuousness and specific-ness of a vivid image – or sound, or smell, or taste, or sensation on the skin – which is created by no more than a few words on a page. A kind of miracle. An ordinary one, because it happens again and again, but miraculous because the few words, clumsy ordinary slabs of the clichéd currency of everyday as they might be, have somehow been touched by a kind of grace that makes them contain more than it would seem possible at face value.

But, because as *readers* of poems we remember the *emotion,* sometimes as *writers* – particularly if we are new writers, or occasional writers – we mistakenly try to name emotions to summon them up. Forgetting that it was the specific-ness of named *things*, and felicitously described *actions,* and the apt detail conjuring a unique event, that evoked emotion. If we become at all abstract, or abstracted, in our writing then we end up at best with 'vague emotions, vaguely expressed'. This introduction, as I write, is killing itself by its desire to generalise. A fatal one, every time.

I am not able to say that such a blurring, or generalising, or naming of emotion rather than conjuring it, absolutely *never* happens in this fecund, yeasty, various collection of work produced in and around writing workshops at the Hen House. But it happens very, very rarely. And after reading the manuscript it's the uniqueness, clarity and excitement of many fragments of lives of girls and women I'm left with. I'm delighted by the confidence – and confidentiality – of these poets to name names, to summon the sharpness and precision of memory rather than the washed blur of nostalgia. There's a truthfulness of experience, an honesty in confronting mixed feelings, a disinclination to blame, an often rueful acknowledgement of complicity which is very moving. And generous. For generosity – of spirit, of language – seems to me the keynote of this thoroughly enjoyable collection.

When Rosaleen Croghan's "Ballagh Girls", none of whom were "... anything but beautiful/or at least had a limp or a hump or died young of TB/or emigrated leaving a crowd of relatives weeping at Kilfree junction" come "back from dances at six a.m. ..." "Dodging their mothers armed with sticks,/meeting Larry Sullivan at the stations of the cross..." the gorgeous garrulousness of rhythm summons up the mother-tongue, the grandmother-tongue of gossiped-about lives which very properly invite our curiosity, indeed our memory, our knowledge of the continuity of women's lives, from whatever culture or context we might, as individuals, come. I pick Rosaleen's poem because it happens to be at the top of the pile in my memory and on my desktop, and because I was so sick of being unspecific I was bursting to quote some . . . For the pleasure of it.

Bathing mothers, burying mothers, learning to love, or at least accept, the deteriorating flesh which gave us life. Exploring sexuality, its shames as well as its sharp pleasures. And writing about it without becoming purple. Flowers, as graphic as Georgia O'Keefe's, as much absolutely themselves and something more than themselves. As in River Wolton's "Lilies" for example. Thanks to Joan Downar, I too can smell "May, Gladys, Edie and Nell". "... their sweet/cheap powder, musky armpits/Edie's hair too thick/for washing much, their best/silk hard with sweat, and/knickers worn a day too long./And soap and broth and pies/And whiskey breath and damp/on bedroom walls/and smoke from cigarettes and fires/and that returning fragrance/from the outside lav." The smell of a very particular time as much as a place, or these persons, May, Gladys, Edie, Nell.

I could quote for ever. But here's the book. I only hope you enjoy it half as much as I did, and you'll be delighted. Congratulations to all the poets included here.

LIZ LOCHHEAD

PRₑFACE

The Hen House was opened in 1987 for women to have a rather splendid country base. But more was to come out of it than just the fun, recreation, and relaxation that had at first been envisaged.

At its best The Hen House has been an extraordinary catalyst and meeting point, where women from a great range of ages, backgrounds, experience, lifestyles and politics found common ground. Networks, friendships and ideas emanated from Hawerby Hall, including the book and international movement called Growing Old Disgracefully.

The West In Her Eye, intended as a memento and tribute to all this, has reflected the Hen House like a mirror image. Like the Hen House, women saw it as unusually accessible and enabling, a truly open forum. Around a third of the contributors never had any work published before, and the rest mostly in local collections. Like the Hen House it is immensely varied, never didactic but with a story to tell. Like the Hen House, it is bringing women together in new associations, looking to further horizons, new visions: the West in her eye...

Like women arriving at the Hen House, the poems I had picked out started to talk to each other. I heard a great buzz of conversation: common themes addressed by different voices, statements and rejoinders, continuities and contradictions, recognition and consolation, until these seven 'ages' emerged – and with them, a new women's publishing venture. The Hen House rides again!

My thanks to all the poets included and also to those who didn't quite make it, to Liz Lochhead and Josephine McCormick for their special contributions, to Barbara Brooks for reading and proofing, to Minnie for managing to keep her paws off the manuscript, and to Sandra, Sue and Carole for their years of support at The Hen House.

RACHEL LEVER
APRIL 1995

CONTENTS

I

little sisters

1. Violets
SUSAN MAYER

Straddling along the dyke,
beneath the surface of the grown-up world
a thin-legged child in flapping wellingtons
squelches through the undergrowth,
intent on pillage.

She grips the razor-bladed grass for balance,
finds her prize,
snip-snaps tender, pale thin stalks,
then licks her palms in glory.

Hugged within her breast,
wrapped in dripping burdock leaves,
booty culled from thick moss walls
– secreted stolen amethysts.

Urchin of the ditch,
she swish-swashbuckles back,
along her green triumphal way,
beating down the whipping nettles,
unseen sapper of authority.

2. Rain
CATHERINE HARRIS

Rain warm and safe inside as it
rattles wildly on the roof.
Cold rain that seeps through your underwear
dripping off eyelashes
and the tip of your nose
Rain falling off lush green
boughs in the garden.

Trees
Bending under the weight
Of rain drops
As big as eyeballs
Wet soaking footprints
across the grass
Traverse
to shake the tree
all over me – wet
webbed eyelashes even
'Catherine come away from that tree'
my mother calls.

I giggle wriggling wet
A rush of pleasure
swamping me
about how naughty
I've been.

3. Girls Convent
POLLY HEYES

Some of the rougher girls
Transposed to boys.
To make a better balance
Of the place.

Jennifer was one,
We all secretly knew.
But nobody would tell her,
To her face.

She lay flat on the grass
Arms flung back,
Hands behind her head,
And didn't care

About the split wide
Side seam of her dress.
That showed the sparkling sweat,
And brownish hair.

The sharp disgust
This caused us as we sat,
Skirts decorously hooked
Over our knees

Helped variegate the days,
Sifted of life.
But no-one ever could,
Pee up the trees.

4. The Edge of Space and Greengage Jelly
CAROLINE ELKINGTON

Darkly curved the convent corridors in chocolate brown,
the squeak of plimsolls on lino,
the smell of incense from the chapel.
Jesus nailed above my bed.
Filing crocodile fashion to the market town,
feeling a fool in white lace gloves and unholy guilt.
Everything neatly arranged in rows;
blazers, boaters, bicycles, girls.
Nuns sliding through shadows deeper than dark
and the carnal, bloody smells from the bacon factory
on Eau-De-Cologne Street,
mingled with the scent of menstruation.
Protected by the Holy Grotto
we swigged sweet cider and puffed dog-ends,
lurking with intent behind Our Lady's secret smile,
spirals of smoke drifting from beneath plaster skirts,
a miracle of sorts.
And at supper Dymphna McGuire said
she would walk backwards barefoot
to the end of the Universe
for a date with Ringo.
Which prompted me to explain my theory
on the edge of space
using greengage jelly.
Infinity is a bugger to unscramble
before double Geography,
on a Thursday.

5. The Ballagh Girls
ROSALEEN CROGHAN

None of the Ballagh girls were anything but beautiful
or at least had a limp or a hump or died young of TB,
or emigrated leaving a crowd of relatives
weeping at Kilfree junction.
They all sent money home to their mothers
and got big jobs or husbands in America.
Or were spectacularly fecund in Northampton,
like Angela Dempsey whom the Lord blest with 17 children.

They spent their school days on their knees
before nuns who had names like the Borgias
for annointing themselves with the red leaves of the
Irish messenger.
The Ballagh girls in a frost of square necked white dresses.
Coming back from dances at six a.m. and hiding their shoes
under the bed
dodging their mothers armed with sticks,
meeting Larry Sullivan at the stations of the cross

The Ballagh girls walking to school in high boots
and black stockings.
Swallowed in the empty mouth of England and America.
Frosted patterns on a bitter glass.

6. Dancing Display
BERNADETTE MARIA CREECHAN

Granny, Mammy, Daddy, Auntie Sadie, oor Wilma, her man
and the stoap-fartin' twins stamp all over the front row,
smokey bacon crisps and Kwenchy Cups eating off
their fidgety faces.
Ssh. Lights down and it's 'Shoop Shoop' here we go.
The curtains shuffle open. Mammy breathes in, Granny taps
her stick, and the twins start their flatulent routine,
the one with triple breaks.
It's showtime again as wee Mary McTavish wings in the
wings, Katy pick-ups her nose and, in her No7 face
Jenny gives it laldy with lurex hips.
Sarah stomps on her glittery feet, stealing her headband
along with the limelight.

The music fades and the curtains struggle shut,
enveloping wee Mary, frozen to the spotlight,
in a splendid velvet cloak. She stumbles, effortlessly,
into the jazz splits,
pulling the curtains along with the house, down with her.

Tinsel garlands tumble down, showering her
to tumultuous applause. The puddle beneath her shimmers
magnificently in silver
and Shirley Temple hasn't got a look-in.

Aye, ma wee lassie's the best wee tinsel lassie,
the best wee dancer, the star of the show,
Ma wee lassie's the best wee tinsel lassie,
The best wee dancer, in Glasgow.

7. The Family
LESLEY MARSHALL

The kitchen was off the living room. No door.
A second floor Glasgow tenement.
Straight ahead an old wooden table,
Covered in blue and white 50s checked fablon,
Score marks through it.
All the household business carried out on it.

Her Uncle scrapes on scrapes off her toast
The Blue Ribbon 'Mary Jane'
With a "ye'll no need both marg and jeely on yer piece".

The doorbell rings
The sound carries, it has to.
The visitor is known,
He frames the doorway,
Tries to buy her smile.
She hands it back
She's nobody's for a shilling.

"Are ye no ready for going up the city the night?" he asks.
Her Uncle makes room on the table,
Finishes shining his shoes,
Then uses it as a board
To iron his shirt front only.

"This is my eldest niece"
Her Uncle explains.
"That's what she's called these days",
The visitor grins his reply.

The racing finished, the TV goes off.
Her Uncle croons a Bing Crosby tune
He must have won,
And tweaks her cheek on the way out.
"Ye'll be a great singer –
Not quite as good as me of course –
If ye keep practising."
He always says that.

8. A Sunday Lunch 1942
JEAN HAMPTON

In Tooting Broadway, London
At three o'clock on Sunday,
My uncle was happily drunk,
In charge of a rusty bike.
Grinning, he held out to my aunt
A galvanised bucket ... full of shit.
"I caught it gal from the shellfish dray"
He tried to say 'Chrysanthemums'.
"For Gawd's sake, put it out the door"
My aunt spat out at him,
As she bulleted the peas in the metal collander,
Knee-cradled in her lap.
In swaying silence, uncle stood,
Viewing the magpie at the end of the yard,
Tick-picking from the pink pig's back.
"If you covered a woman's backside
With treacle and licked it bare,
You'd never please her" he told the sow.

Two days before his pension, uncle died,
On the footplate of a London tram.
As he pulled the bell for Balham
Only his heart stopped.
My aunt hung on the living room wall
A long service bond, and lived on in poverty.
Once a year she cut her prize blooms
Stood them tall on uncle's grave.
And thanked God for their life together.
"A decent man, considering", she gently said.

9. Patterns In The Snow
SALLY ST. CLAIR

Feel the cold as you wake.
Seeping onto your face from behind the curtains.
You know what it means.
You know what the smothering silence means.
There will be drifts of snow across the garden
Burying the rabbit cage, heeled up to the borders.

Outside, the sky is pale and heavy.
The swings have white top hats.
On the lawn, my father has trodden a heart.
Sam and Margy, and kisses.
The boughs of the cedar are weighted to the ground.
At breakfast, my mother's face is still as air.

Down across the deep white plain, snow into the tops of my
Wellington boots, carrying cabbage and burnt toast, I see the
blood before me. Smears of pomegranate pink and scattered
scarlet beads, and all around, the careful dainty elegance of
the fox. I kneel in the silence and slowly push cabbage leaves
into an empty cage.

Twenty years later, my father says,
"That woman was stubborn as a mule."

10. Grandmother
REBECCA MILLER

Roped hands swift
to the sound of
Uncontrolled children.
We stopped our feet
On upstairs landing,
Rammed our mouths
with fists.
She would not need
to mount the stairs
For we would dive
into our beds,
Shut our eyes to
let sleep come.

In the day smell
boiled cabbage drifting
Sticks heavy to walls.
Tinned beans glued
to floppy toast she
rationed us out
our equal shares.
However our births
defined, blood met.

11. Mother
PENNY CHAMP

God lives in the tree she said
As we heard the wind sing through the leaves
And I wondered how she knew such things
As she turned to me and smiled

12. Stories
ALISON GUINANE

Between those covers, mums were good,
convicts merely tied you up,
no-one undressed. When something broke,
a friend could signal Morse Code,
or ride for help. We were kids,
flies on walls. Grown-ups forged Big
Business. (Eat up, Shut up, Don't run,
Get upstairs.) Those men who skulked –
the unwashed, foul-mouthed, brainless thugs,
giving games away till games were up,
with shabby clothes and cockney twangs –
weren't anyone's uncle, anyone's dad.

13. Parlour Song
CATHERINE KLONTZ

Down and out, without a crumb, the children
come to Candy Cottage, hand in hand they
stand, away from home, upon the very
edge of Shady City. Is it pity,
Lady, calls them in? Saves their skin, for whom?
Do you smile and lick your lives as though to
savour some anticipated flavour?

Come my dears, set the table, pay no heed
at all to fable. It's so nice you can
stay, I'm having people for lunch today.

14. Shadowland
LYN BARLOW

Trapped in shadowland
where monsters loom in corners
and screams are soundless whispers
You can't reach me here, teach me how
to tell

What great ears you've got
– but you can't hear me can you?
What great eyes you've got
– you can't see me either?
What great teeth you've got
– but they're not for tearing secrets
are they?

Back in shadowland
I guess this time's forever
I'll learn to scream in silence
Lie still and close my eyes

15. The Poison Child
JACQUELINE FERREIRA

The childhood me
Is a poison elf
That pops up wailing
When I'm least prepared.
I'd burn it in hell
But it's already there.

16. Don't Touch Me
ANNE MAC DARBY

"Let's tickle her to death"

They don't mean it
but they know your Achilles Heel
you're at their mercy
tender, open; they hold down
your kicking legs
tickle tickle
until they reduce you
to a gagging simpleton

Only Father's knee was safe
his pockets good for swapping penknives
blackberries from Grandad's hands
were good to eat
other hands hurt, even the Doctor
cunningly, so Mother doesn't see

Other men threw you too high in the air
men in smelly trousers, damp jumpers
the ones who liked to tickle little girls
their hard hands prodded your body
like they poked cattle at the mart
tickie tickie tickie
big rough hands grab you quick
before you can escape
"poor harmless Tom, don't be such a sourpuss"

Your hurt look pains me
when you reach out suddenly
I stiffen
when you play too hard
my old reflex draws me away
you are confused
can't see all the hands
I am drawing away from

17. Soup Days
JUDITH BRYAN

My mother can't play piano,
Not one whole melodious note.
Nor did she stroke the keys' ebony
On sepia, white of her eye
On teeth of a dead grey beast.
Instead His trouser's belt ruled
And my body ached, for want
Of her orchestration.
Welts rose, fat as worms, wound
Across backs and bottoms and thighs,
Flicked a hot forked tongue
And seared me through: branded CHILD
Across my body.

I carried the scars boldly, I thought,
Sure someone would remark on their ritual splitting:
Seeping pus and blood into my school-desk,
Bursting styes to seal my mouth and eyes.
I felt weighed down with wounds, crucified
To my years, in all ways unclean,
Unclean.
In truth my bell was mute to other ears;
I stooped no more or less than any other child.
Sly as summer moles, my bruises shied
From other eyes, left only
Smooth skin – brown and plump and shiny.

There never was a way to say it.
I glistened, a bright girl in a bright
Heaven; agile to straddle the top rungs
Of the climbing frame.
Eloquent in movement-and-mime.
Quick as a bird in all my lessons.
I laughed, played hopscotch. Had a fat lip
That burst, unfailingly, every winter.
Mine was a happy childhood.

18. The Wooden Spoon
JO PESTEL

The wooden spoon is small and worn
Well worn
From beating and repeating round the bowl
That's old and crazed and blotchy-white.
A silent spoon
Roughened with work.
Smelling faintly of vanilla long ago.
A tongue of wood concave convex
That keeps its counsel of those times
When it became
A wild extension of her arm that held it
Whirled it, angry flailed it through the swishing air
Beating and repeating
And drawing tears.

And in salt silence
Her children licked their bruises.
Not the mixture in the bowl.

19. Five French Verbs
PHYLLIS WALKER

Back in Nineteen Thirty Two
When Young Ladies went to school
Punishment was "Just see me,
Five french verbs, back here at three,
Extra prep, no cakes for tea."

Caught outdoors without a hat
"Against the rules, we can't have that,
Five french verbs, and do not chat,
Wear your hat the whole day long,
Then all will know that you've done wrong."

"Put this book upon your head
Turn those toes out when you tread,
Fold in corners on your bed,
Don't run in the corridor,
Five french verbs, do you want more?"

Found out at break in my houseshoes
"Bring some string and make a noose,
Tie the shoes beneath your chin,
Keep them there for drill and gym,
Five french verbs, then hand them in."

"Did I hear you ate a sweet?
How disgusting, IN THE STREET!
Five french verbs, the tuck shop's out,
Please Young Ladies, do not shout,
The Governors may be about."

20. Whispers From 1929
KIT EVANS

They're always in my head.
Their whispers.
Awakening me in other people's houses,
among other people's possessions.

Iron bedsteads, brass-knobbed.
Flock mattresses.
Ornaments on chests of drawers.
A vest of winceyette. A liberty bodice.
A green gymslip. A cream blouse.
A pair of darned socks. All,
draped over other people's floors.

Furtive feet.
Whispers.
Dressing with fear of fumbling fingers.
Flying with fright.

Downstairs.
Through other people's entrances,
into other people's kitchens.

Mother whispering - "Eat up your breakfast"
I watch her weariness:
Cooking for the sets of the parlour people.

They're always in my head. Their whispers.
"Silence. Or..."

21. May, Gladys, Edie, Nell
JOAN DOWNAR

May, Gladys, Edie, Nell –
I can smell them when I hear
their names, the sticky furrows
down their breasts, their sweet
cheap powder, musky armpits,
Edie's hair too thick
for washing much, their best
silk hard with sweat, and
knickers worn a day too long.
And soap and broth and pies
And whiskey breath and damp
on bedroom walls and smoke
from cigarettes and fires
and that returning fragrance
from the outside lav.
They say our longest lasting
sense is hearing. I
can't hear them, but can smell
May, Gladys, Edie, Nell.

22. War-Time Memory
LUCY NEWSAM

Being alone
Under the table
Caged by bulbous mahogany legs.

Heavy feet
Marching round and round and round;
Hard-toed black hammered leather boots,
Khaki trousers grasped by unyielding webbing.

I fall asleep.
Only to wake, years later,
Still screaming.

23. Once Upon A Summertime
CAROLINE ELKINGTON

Flat on my pre-pubescent belly
up Church Field, aged eleven,
the quaking grasses
in a gothic arch
of bleached ochre
above my head.
Senses swamped
in the hot, musky scent of hay
and parched wild flowers,
their dry-as-moondust heads
embroidered
on a cloudless August sky.
Beetles in irridescent disco green
and raggedy moths
in palest powdered silk,
disturb the muffled air
flustered and directionless,
as, uninvited,
a stranger penetrates
my Lilliputian world.
The snake,
lowdown and sinful,
appraises me
from a cadaver's eye
then slips away
on chain mail skin
through the towering grasses.
The dust settles,
the moths return
and all is the same
but everything has changed.

24. On The Brink
CATRIONA DICKSON

After tea
she took me out
to the circular seat
beneath the apple trees.
Forty degrees at noon
had cooled to thirty,
birds chattered,
crickets purred.

We watched the day
dwindle, the grass
run dark, a plane
scratch the retina of the sky.

She put her hand in mine,
stared stony blue eyes
for a second
then lowered her lids
as I caught the spark.

We were drunk
on summer
we knew we wasted
those final, precious hours
of infancy.

The evening star
glittered like an omen.
Autumn crept up and struck me from behind.

(Dedicated to the memory of Martyn Wiley 1994)

25. Boyfriends
JENNY FIDLER

By the bus stop
uncertain couples
bide their time, cautious
thinking of sex education classes
smothered giggles at serious questions
hand-covered faces, only the eyes to be seen
daring, laughing.

Last lesson; five minutes to freedom
but first we must meet for
that dreaded mouth-to-mouth
      –   wish I could dodge it
            but a fourteen year old
            has her reputation to think of.

Uncomfortably,
an embrace of sorts
Squirm, struggle,
and part.

The pounding has ceased
I am the last, breathless at the bus
relieved at my latest achievement.

26. Mica Cafe
PAULA BURNETT

Beyond the fogged glass of a winter afternoon
taxis like leeches hunch in rows.
The Southern Region's arteries throb below
a thousand beats an hour, weaving Thames to Solent,
the plaid of suburbs to metropolis.

The Gaggia steams and hisses like a train;
spoons jingle decorously when a non-stop rumbles.
The cafe, solid as a dried-out cake of soap,
grows filmy, seems a pasteboard image
marked 'Before' in a designer's folder,
a fifties stageset scrapped for next week's rep.

I sat my adolescence out in bars like this,
pale-foaming coffee spinning like Charybdis
in a Pyrex cup, the handle too small always
for the finger to go through. Steam
crimped my hair to baby-fluff again.

The solid burghers peered in at the sad attempt
to glow and saw hell-fire, giving us credit
for undreamt-of vice. Inside the tank
we mouthed our bubbles in a show of intercourse,
knowing the night rain always waited up.

II

love and lust

27. Let Pleasure
JOAN WOODS

Let pleasure burst through your heart
Let it knock you back
And thrill you with its aftershock
Let it spike down your centre
And your sex
And be happy
As a kebab on a hot skewer

28. On rising from her bed, myself ready to leave.
JOAN WOODS

"Even after our bodies
have turned to dust
and the seas
have turned to tar.

We shall be blood.

Together and apart
you are embedded in me
Flesh of my heart."

29. Apart
CLAIRE PEARSON

through these chill nights
I have held you close,
caressed every contour,
smelled your skin,
tasted you . . .

my love, the miles are
a mere technicality:

in all this time
I never left your side

30. Diptych
ROWENA BARRETT

They say the only thing we do alone
is die. But you in me and I in you,
as mothers in birth, lovers in death,
    we are one.

They say we need a sense of separateness
for symbiosis. Yet you with me and I with you,
midwives in the history of our eternity,
    we are one.

They say the universe is read in silhouette
against a quasar. So you on me and I on you,
shadowed on the edge of dark horizons,
    we are one.

31. For What It's Worth
SARA-JANE ARBURY

you once said
you never
amounted to anything
in your life.
you once said
you never
made it to the top.
Not true.
The heights
You climbed
in my mind
made me dizzy.

32. Lilies
RIVER WOLTON

I couldn't take my eyes off them
in the ferny dankness of the flower shop,
with the baby's breath and innocent anemones
flanking them like Walt Disneys next to a blue movie.

My feet stuck to the floor
like secateurs on a tough rosebush,
locked on the upward thrust of dusted stamens
wanting to be touched.

Her smell still echoed on my fingers
and her pounding in my valleys
leaving the surf on my thighs like high tide moss,
would she think of it too?

Swollen as a green sponge
with last night already stealing from me
in the high-street greyness,
I pulled them from the vase in armfuls.

I could have snapped the stalks
and hurled them in the air,
but I slowly folded them in crimson paper
that quivered as it lay beside the white flesh
like red hot sin on a Sunday.

33. Some Suggestions Concerning You
SARAH CORBETT

The nearness of you is broken summer grasses;
The touch of you the seeding of the air
And our sneezes making cornflowers pollinate.

A whole kitchen is in your smell.
It secretes its ingredients in small places;
Busies itself in the clutter of my tongue and hands.

Your belly is a steamed august pear
Warming the smoothed out cup of my palm,
Giving up the creased hub of its stem to a fingertip.

Your nipples are blueberries ripening in my mouth.
My cheek coasts the raw plantain of your sides;
I play my teeth in the freshly turned hay of your ribcage.

The neat walnut halves of your buttocks
And the small open fruit of the small of your back, are
Cultivating suggestions in the coarse grass of my groin.

34. Love Poem
ROSY WILSON

This morning, love, was like
eating ripe avocado pears,
dressed and seasoned
with olive oil, lemon juice,
basil and black pepper,
spooning towards the centre
where the seed had been.

35. A Hot Poem
TRACY JEUNE

Look boy, you are beautiful – you are hot
I've walked 30 blocks in 20 below
Your face, your body kept me warm
Woa there, I could blow a storm.

You're in me
You're up me
You're all around
I don't think I can make a reasonable sound
I'm hot for you, it hurts me to say,
Eggs over easy, again and again...

My desire is as straight as a New York street,
As rich as Madison
As varied as the Alphabet seat.
I'm urban for you baby
I'm going curb crazy
Look at me, look at me, turn your head
Bite into my Big Apple,
Make us both some soda bread.

Part your lips, part mine too
My sighs are long
My gasps are lewd
How could you ever be so pleasantly confused?

I'm hot for you baby
I'm feeling alright
Let the dark darkness
Disguise us all night

We are two angels, gentle and warm,
trying out heaven, though our earthwings are torn.
We can soar above the Jackson Heights
Just bring me down gently and tuck me in tight.

I'm hot for you, baby
My temperature's rising fast
My head's full of hazy dreams...
Come on, brave one, let's make this one last and last.

36. Can You?
JOAN WOODS

"Can you see me?"
Grinning in the corner of your room.
Side of the eye
Beat of the heart
"You're so beautiful!"

"Can you hear me?"
Coming down your telephone.
Smooth explosions
Shooting city to city
"You're so soft!"

"Can you smell me?"
Sliding over your skin.
Single, sea metal
Honeyed and thick
Taste me NOW!
"You're so sweet!"

"Can you feel me?"
Smiling on your back.
Running through joy
I curl round you and sing
"You're so cool!"

37. Last Tango With Magritte
LYDIA ROBB

My dancing partner's head is webbed in gauze,
his voice is mummified, his eye unseeing.
The picture haunts, I cannot put a face
to him. His mouth is dumb with folded linen.

The space between us shrinks gossamer fine.
The city-slicker in a sombre suit
has laid himself between my silken lines.
The gibbet spins; a tightening in his throat.

He's over-ripe, I peel his mask away.
The kiss of death is tasting how he feels.

Bluebottle sounds of distant summer days
Are coiling round the room. I take my meal.

38. Untitled
JANET KERSEY

Your kisses cover my whole mouth
Slug-eating breath suck by suck
Until I take my only air from you, return it full,
Pulsating in a cocoon of touch.

Needing only you in my lungs,
Your tongue irresistibly drawn to my wet chrysalis,
You lick away the walls of old growth
And my wings beat to the rhythm of your beautiful chest.

Two rib cages
Easing apart
To free
The flight

The tenderest, the hardest, of moments.

39. She Eats Cherries Slowly
KAREN KUEHNE

She eats cherries slowly

allows her tongue to pierce
the red flesh, rolls
the cherry stone across her teeth

She eats cherries slowly

turns the stem round
and round in her fingers as
the juice pools and slides

She eats cherries slowly

examines the stone
before placing it
in the pile beside her.

She eats cherries slowly

while thinking of him.

40. Dumbstruck
GRETA STODDART

The stile stepped over itself
And led me to a boy
With a skull of pale moon,
Orange lips and fishwater eyes.

You, I said.

And a mechanical handful of crows
Argued his name
In rasping black colours.

You, I said again.

Then in dreadful response
His fingers splayed out
In passionate sixes and sevens.
His tongue flipped a beat
Against his swollen lips,

Strumming ancient chords
That shivered in silence.
My superior heart took a blow,
Sweat travelled a tingling moat
Around my hip.

The river ran by
Upturning her silver palms, offering nothing
But a tilted mirror
At the pretending sky that retired
Folding a lilac cloth across the sun.

Then he glanced for one terrific moment
At my birdish throat.
My heart thudded at the wrong rib
And his yellow fingers slid under my skin,
Fiddled there with curiosity
At my sodden folds.

So we rose quietly,
As companions,

.../..

. . . DUMBSTRUCK

Ascending the trees,
Our toes tapping the surprised leaves,
Rising above the earth
That stared up
Open-mouthed.

41. Untitled
AMANDA JAZRAWY

A dress
Forgotten
Surfaces.

Revel in the folds
Of possibility.

You would,
If you
Saw.

Caressing breasts,
Revealing slowly
A valley of
Damp possibility.

Hips beckoning palms
Which can slide
To the unprotected
Folds of thirst.

Artistic creation,
Shadowed,
Lidded,
Natural possibility.

Framing vision.
Framing possibility.

42. Dragon of Desire
CLAIRE MARSHALL

He took over her body.
Finger, nail, elbow, joint.
Swallowing the previous careful woman
into the horn of the jimson flower
white bright
as she screamed YELLOW
for the faceless children
unconceived
for she ran
molten liquid,
fluid down his throat,
vapour to his breath,
particle upon his hide.
For she was RED,
canna red for the Zoccolo monster.
For the papier maché devil
made by idle hands.
Dancing for St Vitus
Frenzy for St Anthony.
Flame tongue, she was GOLD,
marigold, flower petals to her opening womb
of his sister, of his wife,
of his daughter not yet cold
inside her grave,
warming to his sex.
Dragon of Desire.
He took over her body.
Time to burn.
He took over her mind.
She was glory.
Morning Glory.

43. A F . . . ing Haiku
ANNE GARNER

Stimulation with
copulative ecstacy
beats masturbation.

44. Forbidden Fruit
DIANE HICKMAN

That was the time . . .
Oh, I can't tell you
It felt so good.

We'd visited a friend
And talked of love all night . . .
There were some wandering eyes.
Eyes which knew breasts.
Eyes which widened at the thought
Of hardened nipples,
Moistened lips following a trail of kiwi fruit,
Mapping unfamiliar land . . .
Familiar – unfamiliar.

We laughed so much –
The realisation of our passions.
For the years we'd touched each–other with care,
Now we touched in lust.

All night like violins we,
In turmoil,
Crescendo after absolute fulfilment.
"no more" we vowed.
And with our hunger,
Turned to more edible lusts.
We ransacked the kitchen,
As hastily,
As greedily.
"Eat what you want, I am."
We tittered like children,
Slapping our bare feet around the quarry tiles.
Pinch your sandwich and steal a kiss . . .
Oh I want you.

So juvenile,
We ordered each–other
To opposite corners of the room,
To breathe, to eat . . .
We hurried – you finished first,
And came for me, monster–handed – Creeping.

.../..

. . . FORBIDDEN FRUIT

I crammed my sandwich, whole, into my mouth.
I was Fay Wray – you were King Kong.
I pressed my fists up to my nose,
My breasts together with my fore-arms
Pretending to scream.
Eyebrows raised.

– A mischievous thought.

45. Round Words, Square Ears
GILLIAN ROWAN

When the talk at a dinner party
turns to love, and a
lively woman turns
silent.
Do not assume
do not assume
she has no tale to tell.
Chances are, that woman walks the flipside,
and unspilled words are brimming.
Rollicking, rounded, curvy words,
that would jam in the frames of
square ears.
Don't they even
notice
the still of her face, her
smoothed, politely glazed, face?
Oh, she would talk if they would hear,
but there's little point till they
bend their ears.

46. "Landscapes Like Sleeping Women . . . "
ANDREA BURGESS

Moving beneath the sheets she
shifts, like the neap tide
washing drifthoughts ashore
on the beach of my imagination.

She is sleeping, and
I cannot, I lie awake
and think of wandering
over hillsides, finding fresh
pure springs of water.

Earlier we talked, she
told of her adventures, she
explored the Amazon forest.
With her sweet mouth she
described beauty.

47. On Visiting An Ex-Lover's Flat for a Meeting
KATE HALL

I am no longer present
dismissed
no card bears my name
no photograph my image
no small reminder
to say we ever touched
I have been removed
from your life
and your notice board
resplendent with lovers and friends.

A disorderly foible
that began to collect dust
on your carefully arranged shelves
and was, for convenience sake
quickly tidied away.

48. If I Please You
VALERIE LOUDON

Don't roll away and fall asleep
And snore the way you do.
Remember afterglow, my love,
And please me, please, if I please you.

49. Lover
ANNA WALKER

I held him last night,
While he was fast asleep.
He didn't even notice.

I took his hand,
I kissed his palm,
But he rolled over.

I could feel him next to me,
His warmth seeping through.
I woke up this morning,
In the arms of my lover.

50. First Time
ANNE GARNER

Her smile
licks its lips
like
the cat with the cream;

his cream, poured
into a vessel
shaped for their delight.

Kitten like she purrs
and dreams
whilst he swaggers
in tight jeans,
like a pride of lions.

51. Loose Ends
JUNE ENGLISH

'Relax, with legs apart, this won't take long,
Ah! Nurse, a kidney bowl, she's feeling sick.
That's it, well done, now I'll dress your sun-burn,
It's quite severe, lie still, you'll feel the prick . . .'

We lay entwined beneath the biting sun,
Our rhythmic breathing merged with swelling sounds
Of surf that cooled our burning feet. His mouth
Exploring, found and sucked, at ripened-rounds

Of fleshy bum-cheeks. "Luscious fruits are best
If eaten warm," he whispered. Panting I
Succumbed as passion's flame subsumed me . . .
We parted – two loose ends – without a tie.

The Doctor burst the biggest blisters first:
'My dear, I think you're pregnant. Rest
At home awhile. I'll let you know for sure,
When I receive results of the urine test.'

52. Isolated Incident
SALLY CLINE

I thought the thought of you would be enough.
Having had you . . an unsound phrase . . just the once.
Quite sufficient.

"We must not make commitments". You said that
in a trice. Now imagination will suffice.

I thought the thought of you would be enough.
Having seen you . . with . . as they say . . the naked eye.
The naked what? Spilling over my naked shaking self.
Not once but twice. Now imagination must suffice.

I thought the thought of you would be enough. I
have your photo. I have read your card. I have carefully
reduced the risk of attaching any value, or settling any
price, on . . .

Imagination will suffice.

I thought the thought of you would be enough. I
thought we might try and turn it into Good Solid
Friendship. I thought . . .

Screw thinking! It is you I want.

53. Night On The Zambezi
RUTH HARTLEY

The mosquitoes have tattooed
my defending knuckles
with 'LOVE' and 'HATE'
and etched the ululating air around my head
with thin wails of grief.

I cannot sleep.
The round obsessive moon has ironed
my brain as bland and flat as her mad jealous face
and gentle dreaming will not stick to it.

I am the sweating night's prisoner
and the sun's rejected child.

Sleep and my lover have left me
and there is no hope of this night ending.

54. Sparks
JENNY MORRIS

Emma is earthbound.
Her gaze is direct.
She can wire a plug,
looks good in green and yellow,
is contained, composed.
Fell for a blues band singer
felt the current.
She the top terminal
he the neutral on the left
watching in a corner.
For weeks said he loved her.

Until he connected
with the live wire
on the right, the one
with the fast fuse,
red high heels, long dark hair
all over the place.
The opposite, that's what hurt.
He spoke to Emma
with his face turned away,
adapting, disconnecting.

55. The Next Customer
JUDY KENDALL

My fear of intimacy
Means I dart and dive
Twixt man and dream
Always looking for
The next customer

And when I sense
We're getting close
I'm always quick
To whip out
My pocket calculator
And ask how much

56. Natasha And The Birds
JENNY MORRIS

Like dead fledglings, she thinks,
plump stippled corpses of dropped
hibiscus flowers
clammy, purplish, veiny.
Can't pick them
off the floor
because her flesh creeps.
Natasha from Georgia
makes men pay, never lets them
kiss her on the lips,
blocks her chimney in case
a bird comes down,
won't walk near pigeons,
remembers her mother's hands
fluttering behind bars.
Natasha, marsh mallow woman
never puts silent trumpets
of hibiscus in her hair.

57. Morning Sunlight
LUCY ROBESON

I dreamt we were walking
Across a snowy field
Morning sunlight everywhere
We were climbing over fences
And I think we were hand in hand
And I was dressed in red
And you were dressed as a man
And then we started running
And sliding on the ice
And I don't remember any gunshots
but suddenly we were on the ground
And I don't remember any blood running
but we were dissolving into morning

So cold

58. Too Fleeting Vision
ANNE MAHER

All at once and unannounced
your face appears before my eyes
in darkened rain-drenched window panes
or on the pages of a book
beneath my halting pen.

And as I scrutinise you there
you fade and disappear once more
and I am left with blinded eyes
that have to take a sideways look
to catch a glimpse again.

59. Loving You
SHEILA SMITH

Precarious handhold, loving you,
fending off fear, small stones
plummeting, earth crumbling
to rocks idling below.
I took the moments
level eye to eye, spilling one life
into another, prodigal, satisfied.
We could lie silent and speak volumes
hands' touch closer than linked steel;
or a gully sank open sheer and wide
no hope of getting near, except I tried.

I manufactured festive days, insisting
on celebration. You eluded life
in death. The room was shrilly
silent, the phone's ear-piece
deaf in my hand. Staring from
desolation's bed at the window's
presiding pallor at the gently gathering
darkness to make out your presence
there.

60 For Mona
HELENA AKSENTIJEVIC

"I will call you Bhabi – my brother's wife"
You said,
And took me by the hand and led me
To the roof to tell me secrets.
Then I danced for you and
You threw back your head, laughed.
For a moment,
Your beauty rivalled the Indian sun.
That night I remember we told each other stories,
Lying in that double bed.

So many things I'd like to tell you.
I wish that I had written you letters
I wish that we had got together,
Most of all
I wish you weren't dead.

61. Cafe And Love
ELIZABETH BEX

All day long I sat
as if obsessed
with the thought
that I might see you

My eyes were watching
like the eyes of a window
and I fantasised
the meeting

The sounds in the cafe
were almost numbing
and my thoughts returned
to music and dancing

Late into the night
only the cinema screen
mirrored my feelings
and my tears cried

One suicide is just
like another
and I choked on the grief
that I was still alive

62. Numbed
TISH OAKWOOD

war wife
husband killed
overwhelming
hysterical grief of the woman
left with life

      O
      to love a man enough
      that you cared
      whether he lived
      or died.

63. Laughter
AUDREY HAMILTON

Laughter is my happiness now far away
And laughing in another place
With some unknown conspirators.
I was there; I did not know
When tightly creased lines around eyes
And mouth engulfed me too
That laughter's pain in the belly
Would move around my heart and mind
And feel like sorrow
Remembered through a lapse of time
Now lacking spontaneity of smile . . .

Facades of smiles;
Can one sift the changing patterns of contours
On a visage of experiences
To discern truths?
I did not know when I was there
Of other far off imitations pending.
A smile may hide emotions unexpressed;
A silent face may yet foretell the joy
Of two hearts joined in love and spontaneous laughter.

64. You Safely Boarded . . .
ANNE-MARIE MAPLE

You safely boarded
I just missed the boat
Left stumbling along the shoreline
As you reach out from the stern
Now the last desperate lifeline is thrown
And I cling on for security
Only to be dragged in your wake
Miles out of my depth

65. Quantum Love
KATE SCARRATT

the universal magician, the atomic particle
can be two things at once, think of it,
both waving wave smoothing between two slits,
and a speck of real stuff
a crumb a grain a fragment a bit.

Such effortless duplicity!
a wave when it's waving
but when it hits,
a particle again, real as grit,
this is a sly deceiver:
at the moment of change
cannot be detected
alters when it alteration finds,
changes if it's inspected.

I say that love
is a quantum trick
sliding like a wave when it slides
but grit when it hits
the heart knows how to be
both gritty and slick.

66. Free Wills
JOAN WYATT

He can decide
For truth or lies
But not what she'll believe.

Trust and deceit
Themselves defeat:
Trust once declined
Deceives.

She may decide
For lies and lies:
Her trust a counterfeit.

67. Secrets
WENDY GREENWOOD

Bloody secrets.
Bloody lies.
Protectors?
Appeasing one person.
Destroying another.
Deception.

68. Five Words
DESIRÉE PAULL MERRIDEN

Passion
Desire
Obsession
Fire
Liar.

Damn you, Nigel.

69. Untitled
PIPPA GWILLIAM

Yes, I wanted more.
I bubbled with desire
which sent my blood riotously
through the roof of my restraint,
opening the hearts of stars
to my gaze.
But coming to under a dark sky
my mouth was full of sparks and ashes,
which I swallowed without demur,
grinning a black and silver grin.

70. Loving You
ALISON HOMEWOOD

Loving you is like . . .

Enjoying a wonderful meal,
the finest champagne,
and then –
Yours are the fingers
down my throat.

71. Threnody For The Dead Cow
LAURA POTTS

This Sunday
has layered greys
piled heavy on the horizons,
pulling away, pushing close,
and March winds
whipping brassy new willow stems.

A familiar track
falls away through water meadows
to that summer
in urgent and exuberant delight.
        And memory folds a broad pleat
           now/then
        with sharply ironed precision.

We'd burned away on the motorbike
  old Superdream
restless with desire,
to sit close to close
melting at the joinings,
and in the high afternoon heat,
and from the riverbank,
watched molten water
coiling, langourous.

So I say, in this wry dry time,
        do you remember?
        that summer afternoon, new in love?
And she replies no, and no:
then, as afterthought –
'was that when we saw the dead cow?'

What can I say but yes?
remembering too;
how it had floated past,
swollen, slowly twisting.
        This then the mutual memory,
        pleats shaken out to
        soft creases worn loosely
        against this chill pewter day.

72. In The Darkroom
PAT BORTHWICK

In the red glow of the darkroom
Where the luminous clock ticks on
And stark chemicals slop
In their trays,
Is where I first fixed you.

And now it's plain to see.

I hadn't looked at you before like that,
Afraid you might catch me at it,
But there you were, emerging
From between the borders of wet prints,
Your dark eyes first, like moths
Darkening until clearly defined.
Then that smile, that half smile,
That mouth opening
With words I thought I'd heard you say
But could have been wrong
Seeing how your gaze is fixed
Vaguely above the horizon
And not on me.

This one of Duke has come out well.

73. Wallpaper Girl
EMMA HOOPER

The darkened drizzle of an early morning.
Headlights in puddles, moments
before tyres distort them. Self-absorbed
postmen, milkmen begin their work.

Going back: the vivid blue eyes
drawing a wallpaper girl out at a party.
Attraction grew into an affair. Ending
when, alone one night, you met someone else.

74. Eye
SUE KLAUBER

Caught a woman's eye
sitting in a couple,
blond streaked hair and compassionate eyebrows.
To his horror she felt his gaze,
Peeping Tom at the marital window,
Habitat flat, interesting jobs and thinking about children
he thought.
He stared hard at the ice-cream menu,
relieved when his came.
Creamy mess,
strawberry breasts
burying face between their softness
smooth against his cheeks and
feeling his penis harden.

She walked in with her dull companion
any date was better than no date,
she reasoned.
Getting dressed up
red lipstick and a tight top
breasts firm in her new bra.
Then noticed a good-looking man
pretending not to look at her,
eyes on his cutlery, only permitting a blinkered look
at the waitress.
Then she lost him
to an ice-cream.

75. Farewell
GUIA K. MONTI

The lingering presence of your smile
Haunts the grounds
By the pond
Where the little fish stare up
Aware of the tender crumbs
Of a disintegrating love.

76. Find Me A Shoulder to Cry On
TERI GREGORY

Find me a shoulder to cry on,
Lend me your love.
Buy me a bottle of rainbows,
A branch for a dove.

Sell me a sense of adventure,
Travel with me.
Carry in me, with a fortune of silver,
Sailing the sea.

Drift in me seasons of splendour
Where treasures of old
Are concealed in a tower which crumbles to dust
When daylight grows cold.

Burst in me bubbles of beauty which linger
The night long.
Write for me words that will weep not in tears
But play in a song.

Save me from shadows which stray in my soul
At the end of the day.
See in me freedom and dreams that I share,
If only one way.

Find in me feelings that break out in flames,
Sharp as a thorn.
Tender me true when I say I love you
And when I'm forlorn.

77. Some Small Attention
LESLEY TOWNER

You have played games with me,
tempted my involvement,
touched my vulnerability,
then left me to ferment
in the doubts of myself.

You have caught me unawares,
sown the seeds of interest,
and then abandoned
the harvest.

I can only ask myself,
is this deliberate,
or the result
of your own confusion?

And I may have to suffice
with knowing I was worth
some small attention,
at some point in your life.

78. Learning Curve
KATE SCARRATT

honourable Hector
trusting to the honour of lesser men
disarmed.

poor Cressida, silly cow,
did much the same.

oh, the better part of everything,
I tell you
the better part of everything,

is discretion.

79. Two Cats And A Desk In The Kitchen
WENDY RICHMOND

That first evening she gave me the family bit,
solid, I thought
    very grounded, her with her razzamatazz life, sending out
because she never learnt to cook, two jobs,
a night life worth envy
    and regular four hour spins to hit the weekend surf.
I declined to see the sights, knew I had to get
stuck in
    knuckle down and produce enough before going back
to children, soaps and the local on Wednesdays.
    She goes, hair free to the wind, long mac flapping
as she faces it full. I hadn't grasped the lengths
to which she needed
    to seem healthy, strong, weighted as she was.
I liked the way she didn't once refer to her figure,
or let an inch pass
    before moving on to discuss subjects that suited.
I watch from the window, then warm my back
against the radiator.
    When I first got ill she was all confession, a sickly child,
her mother vengeful from lounge to kitchen
how kids ruin your life.
    Saw then how she clasped her hands,
    clicked her thumbnails,
the even smile, and the way she so very carefully
paced her steps
    And how once, just once, dropped her knife when I joked
about training the kids for my dotage. And I
understood why
    she couldn't ever spend a life with mirrors, domesticity
and the shadows of the cage of a singular place
she never much lived in
    a flat with two cats and a desk in the kitchen.

80. Life After You
ROSELLE ANGWIN

Life after you

is what I'm thinking of tonight.
A small frost falls. Wood spits
and hisses, and the corner-light

shows shadows where an hour ago
you sat, and sadly smiled
and kissed me once, and stood to go.

I still don't know exactly what
you said, or why you went;
or why your absence rips apart

my evening, leaving hollow words
in corners, like dead leaves,
or storm-tossed wingless flightless birds

that stumble and yet try to rise.
Or perhaps I stumble
trying to make sense, to surprise

my heart out of its numbness.
You did not say the words
I feared the most; why then darkness,

death to a million points of light
at once?   –   Life after you
is what I'm thinking of tonight.

81. Water
GENEVIEVE YIP

After this gate gets to close
      I want to keep
my past
away from my running present.
  I have no fear
      only hate
and I am bereft of any emotion
towards that great chamber
               behind this gate.
So remember to keep it shut
for then I was dead
and now, now I am alive.
      Smoke me into a parfum bottle
and hang me around your
neck.
Hey!
      Remember me?
  I was the one who awoke in your arms
dressed real nice
            In jade blue–green seaweed
and white as painted sky.
  Emptied of fears and sickness
till you breathed life into me
           again.
Oh, that was your time to seize!
The mistake has left me alone
      And alone I am understood to be
where nature and death are one
and blood and cement are free.

82. Poems Like Unsent Love Letters
SARAH CORKHILL

When I fell
I wrote of the slow motion pain
the tight coil of unrequited love,
Framed moments on paper
like photographs of frozen feelings.

When we tried
To exchange something of ourselves
I recorded the hit and miss,
push me pull me,
she loves me, she loves me not,
of fresh nervous need.

When we became platonic lovers
I scribbled like a born-again teenager
Hallucinating on fantasies
Of forbidden female fruit
offered in the dark
My hormones ripe for the picking.

When we parted
I scrawled like a wise old woman
of moments in the rain
of my sleepless nights
grieving for all my old loves
As of children who had finally left home.

The need to write it down has been so strong
like catching the light of a beautiful day on film
As if it is proof that I was there
That I was loved
Yet the more I wrote, the more we disappeared.

So now I re-read my emotional graffiti
and I can hardly see the loveliness at all
It is as if it had not occurred
but was only an affair with words
and cannot be rewritten
or the passion returned.

.../..

. . . UNSENT LOVE LETTERS

And I grieve all over again
for a loss of love
more deadly than death,
until in the calm of my exhaustion
I embrace all the words between women
that have made me what I am,
And wonder how many more times
I will re-write the same poems?

83. Poppy Fields
SARAH JANE LUCK

His face is a stone wall.
He will not let me in.
For though I beat the door
With weapons of guilt,
I am but a crack,
On a smooth
And rounded shell.

I did not cradle him,
The inner child to stroke.
But spat out anger
My frustrations so to ease.
For love denied me,
Found no common ground,
But lay,
Amongst Poppy fields.

84. the lanced heart
CLARE FEARNLEY

so maybe
the lanced heart
still beats
still pumps the blood
exchanging old blood
for new

but it does not
leap into the mouth
sprightly & hopeful
bellowing yes
in a wordless whisper

85. Sign Language
ALISON STOKES

At one. And still at war.
You will always be blameless.

The enchanter
Who closed the ears of the air

Who became a connoisseur
Of deafness

But who taught me nothing
Of sign language

Or of how to read lips.
Perhaps I am the lucky one

Even in silence
You swore you heard words.

86. Your Puppet
AMBER

I have written many ballads
Verses and recitals,
Praising the beauty of your face.
But none have expressed
how screwed up with
anger
it could look;
Every time I spoke out of line
or acted out of line
or just simply did not
follow your shadow
In Iambic 1,2 time.

87. Three Unspoken Words
HELEN SHAY

It was over.
After the black rows
And red sex,
I gulped down
The soon solitude
And said it.

'Don't tell me
What I feel'
He denied, pounding
With heavy fist
On the armchair
Of humble inheritance

In that blow
My life fell
Under the hammer.
Offer and acceptance,
A concluded contract
Of irrevocable union.

88. Lost Friendship
RUTH ATHRON

I was sorry
and I felt great pain,
But knew not how to resurrect
The dream I'd slain.
Oh, dearest friend!
My heart would only mourn,
And could not lay aside its pride
To let love be reborn.

89. A Happy Poem
RUTH STOTT

"Why don't you write a happy poem?" you said.
So I wrote your name.
That's a poem that makes my heart sing.
"You and I love each other."
That was another.

Some poems last longer than others.

90. Post Coitum Triste
CLAIRE HEWITT

I feel the wrinkles roll out like pastry
Under a gentle rolling pin.
A smile curls at the corner of my mouth
Like a cat's with a saucer of cream.
For a moment there is perfect happiness.
'Do you feel wicked?' he says
As we lie in a state of suspension.
'I feel happy' I say, 'not wicked at all.'
But as I speak the guilt descends.
He has put me in my place.

91. The Signposts Were There All The Time
PENELOPE SIDNEY

My lover came from Scotland.
  He climbed mountains in his head.
He guided, warmed and nurtured me
  Till I took him to my bed.

My lover came from Scotland.
  He climbed mountains in his head.
He said he'd teach me how to climb
  And show me where to tread.

My lover came from Scotland.
  He climbed mountains in his head.
But when he'd conquered all my peaks
  He remembered he was wed.

My lover came from Scotland.
  He climbed mountains in his head.
He wanted me to follow him –
  But I got there first instead.

92. Perfect Husband
ALISON HOMEWOOD

Fuck the mistress.
How ironic.
Cards on the table,
the triangle's chronic.
One has to go and it won't be the wife.
Supportive, kind and very nice.
Always the one to be acknowledged,
the mummy bear who makes his porridge.
Her husband's a cheat,
isn't ignorance bliss?
As she proffers her cheek to accept
His kiss.

93. The Affair Ends
KATE DURIE

He rings her at two in the morning.
He has confessed everything;
He will come to her. She is scared.
If she wins, can she lose?
She doesn't sleep; spends the day
Washing sheets, baking bread. She tries
Six newsagents for his favourite paper.

He moves in with two spare shirts.
She irons them, places them perfect
On padded hangers in her ex's clattering wardrobe.
Two nights and one day later, they have never
Been so together. The phone rings.
His wife threatens to slash her wrists.
In the background, his son's small cries
Beg for needs like a stray cat.

He says he must go home;
'Home' slices like a new knife.
Its brightness dazzles; you believe your mastery
And chop, chop, chop, until you miss and bleed.
He must just sort this out. Back in two hours.
She waits eight. He cannot meet her eye:
She throws his shirts at him, and they flap
Emptily, birds maimed taking wing.

At night she finds his abandoned jumper;
She cradles it like a newborn mother,
Sniffing her child.
She will not bathe and unmagic his scent from her.

He rings to say he loves her but.

After a week she washes the jumper.
In water too hot it shrinks;
But all her things are a faded, dirty blue,
And the stain will not come out, ever.

94. Retrospect
DAPHNE PHILLIPS

I know when you have been here;
There are luxury left-overs in the fridge
And flowers in the living-room.

I know when you have been here;
There are extra pillows in my bed
And all my towels smell of Antaeus.

I know when you have been here;
I hug these exuberant bruises to myself
And my lips are tender.

I know when you have been here;
The stairs seem suddenly much steeper.

And isn't the clock running down?

95. The Other Woman
JOAN DOWNAR

She looks in the mirror
and doesn't see herself. She sees
abandonment, a woman
sweating with lust, about to take off
to no-man's, no-woman's land.

She whispers: "I am a mistress"
and packs her adulterer's kit:
lies and evasions, justifications.
One day she'll accommodate
the tortured heart, but not now, not yet.

96. Compromise
LAURA HAMILTON

She spits out his guilt in triumph,
with words I'm trying not to hear.
Swelling doubts sprout roots and flower,
battered pride makes way for fear.

Stilled by shock, no breath for crying,
silent pictures fill my head.
I see her lips upon his body,
I see her body in my bed.

A mother's duty to her children
deadens my murderous intent.
A proper childhood has a father,
a proper wife is lenient.

97. The Silent Phone Call
WENDY HOLBOROW

This morning I dialled your number.
You answered, gruffly at first, as is your manner.
Then more gently, then gentler still.
I hung up, afraid I would speak.
I felt you knew it was me on the line,
By the increasing gentleness in your voice.
Our daughter came into my room for a cuddle.
I wept: "don't cry mummy" she said.
And she kissed me, so I wept more.

98. Still Life
ANNE GILLIAM

Warm kitchen,
Winter dawn.
Cat in the window,
Hunched in ginger fur.
Cold twitterings
Of early rising birds;
Breakfast on the table,
Fruit in the blue bowl,
Coffee and toast
To banish sleep.

The dark sky lightens;
Wrapped in shared thoughts
We do not need to speak;
A lifetime together
Has brought us to
This still point,
Mind expanding,
Transcending common day.

99. Loss Of Feeling
TISH FARRELL

Shall we still love when we are old? Or will
The bitter gall of welling disaffection
Seep and spread its crust on once soft flesh; the
Nestling shafts of garnered irritations
Accrete into a bony carapace;
And we retreat, each within our pales, the
Heart of us gone out to husk, which might well
Be our funeral wrap, for all the good of
Living dead. And is this the price we pay
To shut out pain? To fend off grief of loss?
I would not pay it! And I pray to God
To spare us from this mean demise, a lingering
Death by passionless embrace; the small
Contempt of dry lips on an unresponding face.

100. Old Love
CHRISTINE SAGAR

We make love now when half awake.
In deeper sleep our hands and thighs may touch,
Making us turn in tenderness, surprise, such
Hopeful, joyous expectations rise
But then we slowly come to realise
We are not strangers and we know too much.

101. Beautiful
ANDREA BIRD

Tell me I'm beautiful

Not with words, a perfunctory kiss,
But with your eyes, your heart,
With a lingering look,
A hungry clasping, an electric heat.

Tell me I'm beautiful
And I'll dance in your dreams,
I'll weave silken threads through the ice of our sheets.

> Why wait till I strip
>   *Invit. Only*
> before letting your hand
> stroke, briefly, my breast.
> Does my body not move you, arouse or interest?
> Is your castle so buttressed
> None may mount?

A swallow nests in the eaves of your life,
Fly with her, chase her through sunkissed mornings
She's yours for the taking,
For the telling she's beautiful
Lover, love her,
Let her love you
And please,

Tell me I'm beautiful.

102. Marriage Lines, or
Two Monologues Don't Make a Dialogue
PAT TEMPEST

You used to be so kind in many ways . . .
And my reward was love and kisses . . .
You're just not nice to me these days.

I bring you flowers in gorgeous sprays
I think I must have halitosis . . .
You used to be so kind in many ways . . .

We go to lots of concerts, films and plays . . .
Our social life's amazing – never ceases . . .
You're just not nice to me these days . . .

To hell with concerts, films and plays
I'd rather have some love and kisses . . .
You used to be so kind in many ways . . .

I can't believe it's really you who says
my problem's middle aged neurosis . . .
You're just not nice to me these days . . .

There's no need for emotional displays
You're not my sweetheart now, you are my missis . . .
And not so kind in many ways
You're just not nice to me these days.

103. Hook Line And Sunk
JULIE ASHTON

Living with an angler
would try the patience of a saint.
A clean and practical hobby
It certainly aint.

Hooks are found in slippers
fishing wire tangled around feet
and when you open the fridge
goodness knows what you're going to meet. . .

104. Leaving Cornwall
SALLY YOUNG

This time tomorrow
I'll have eaten croissants.
You'll be here.
With the boys. Alone.

You're hardly aware
There's emotional tension.
My creation.
As I am.

Downstairs I'm drawn
To your casual fashion.
Rivulets root
A brimming smile.

They scar all
Outward calm with
Drama. They field
A cautious frown.

Filling time again,
You revise the car.
I cannot
Comprehend it.

All that matters
Is I'm free
To go. I don't
Expect to explain it.

105. The Seal/Nick
URSULA DUNNETT

Your friendly face bounces on the waves
Half-hid;
You're quite curious – at a distance –
About strangers.

You love new tricks – balance on your nose
A black ball –
Sporting and cavorting delights you
In any game.

Not a land animal, in the warm sun,
Heat-hazy,
You flop your rubbery lubber
Onto the rocks.

Coiling and streaking through fronded shoals.
The flashing fish
Are an adventure: you trap them gently
In your soft mouth.

But your whiskers belie you:
Under your frolics, you're a family man.

106. Skin Deep
CLARE FEARNLEY

He wears his black leather waistcoat
like a second skin
maybe to protect himself
as his first skin is too thin

maybe to show that
he has many layers

You want to touch it,
you do yet you don't –
the black dead skin
and the white.

107. Young Buck
RUTH McCLAUGHRY

She went to the pub
to look for him.
He came swaggering out,
young buck,
god's gift to women.
As beautiful now as the day he had married her
to his tasks.

He glanced with a laugh
at her belly,
swollen with pregnancy.

108. Black & Blue Blues
VANESSA WATTS

I feel so trapped with nowhere to go
I feel so down and my spirits so low
Why these bruises so black and blue?
I only wish I had a clue.

My life in turmoil and so much hurt
He often treats me just like dirt
Constant blackmail I can't stand
I wish I had a helping hand.

I feel so trapped with nowhere to go
I feel so down and my spirits so low
Why these bruises so black and blue?
I only wish I had a clue.

109. Possession
PAULINE WRIGHT

You took the person out of me
When I became your wife
You took me as a possession
But still I had a life

You took away my confidence
And trod me into the ground
You took away my right to speak
So I didn't utter a sound

You took away my freedom
And had me tied in chains
You took away my chances
When you controlled the reins

You took and then betrayed my trust
I was not allowed to choose
You took it all for granted
And I was the one to lose

You took away a part of me
That's lost and I can't find
You nearly took my sanity
Playing games with my mind

You took my children's innocence
We were under your spell
You took the best years of their life
And put us all through hell

None of this was yours to take
And I can never forgive
If I could take one thing from you
It would be your right to live.

110. Sweet
V.G. LEE

"Don't fret, don't push too hard,
Sweet girl".
Jaw held so
In bruising hand,
Wet forehead pressed
To tear stained lips.
"No talk, or word,
Not a peep out of you,
When I say smile, remember
Smile."

"One by one,
I could snap
Each little sweet, sweet bone.
Tear you like thick cloth
Through knot and muscle,
Hook hot conduit.
Rasp across red ridged veins
Where blood diffuses.
I could have the time of my life."

"Remember this,"
He says,
"Outside this silence –
Well and good;
Inside; deaf and blind,
You dance to the rhythm
I tap out."

111. Half-Life
DOREEN REYNOLDS

People said you were well-suited,
but your wife has gone –
well-suited to another.

Your personal assistant
does not understand
how well she understood.

You bang your skull
on floor and door.

Your parents' silver wedding: people say
"Why does he drink so much?" You know the joys
will pass when you pass out.

Here is your degree, down from a
clear blue sky, but you distinguish
the clouds, man-sized.

You bang your skull
on floor and door.

At the black shadow of 'No'
falling across your hands –
(hair was for pulling)
your eyes grow dark and wet
your mouth drooping.

You bang your skull
on floor and door.

Each step of your father's pacing
deplores your birth. On a slug bus
your mother, sweating, crosses town,
the milk spurting.

You mouth at your father's sleeve
as if at a dry stalk
under the blenched sky.

112. St. George's Fair
JANET DEAN

A feast of oil-tossed olives,
of cheese and scones.
The moor, a thick brown suede,
brushed by weak Easter sun.
Hot and invertebrate,
you melted round his knees.
Shining and cold
he dressed his smile in steel.

St. George's Fair, all spinning rides,
high Ferris wheel.
His rumbling midnight voice,
below the squeals,
wrapped us like a rug.
I thought of monsters
and nightmare dreams,
you thought of love.

When later his genes
left the print of his rage
on each of your cheeks,
I remembered that day.

113. Watching
JACQUELINE FERREIRA

I'll be watching you sounds like Hollywood –
Until mindless fists beat the barred front door
And crazed feet pound along the hallway floor.

What I'd really like people to have known
Is words double the pain of punches alone,
And that violence never didn't mean it,

Even when the slut deserved just that kind of thing.

114. Internal Injuries
FIONA CURNOW

Let him kiss me with the kisses of essential violence.
I have a hot-wired brain and pain
Secretes its own amphetamines.

The neighbours will not hear my screams
Because I do not scream.
Friends will not see my bruises
Because there are no bruises to be seen:
I have consented.
I am my own best mutilator.

Each day a fresh incision in my reason
Underwrites our love.

115. Fernando's Circus
(After Toulouse-Lautrec)
LIZ ARDEN

Fernando's filly circles
the innocent sawdust –

he whips her with his lower lip,
the curl of his moustache,
his body arch;
her scarlet smile does not demur.
She strains to keep her seat,
dare not look away.

The grey mount bounds her round,
her tulle fantail flies.

The eyes of the upright gentlemen
lick her legs;
they do not enjoy
the clowns.

116. Safe (For Jackie Hill)
ROSIE GARLAND

Jackie and I sat like bookends in the tutor's office.
Her hair was short and brown, mine long,
and she wore glasses.
Our assignments, if unexciting, were always in on time
and we wore dark coats with hoods and collars
to keep out the rain.
We walked straight home.

My shoes were flat and comfortable.
My hair, brushed flat and not provocative.
I spent a lot of time with my eyes pinned to the floor.
My clothes were shapeless.
My boyfriend liked them, told me I was laughable
in anything tight.
I was engaged.
Mum and Dad loved him.
And singing? I hadn't sung for years.
There were more important things to do now.
A whole youth to put behind me.
And each night he had sex with me
I was glad it was dark so he couldn't see my eyes
and guess I'd gone away.

Jackie and I sat like bookends in the tutor's office
and we would walk straight home.
We wore flat shoes.
We did not sing.
We kept our eyes down.
We walked straight home.

And one Monday night,
while I sat neatly tucked in a happy foursome
watching the second reel of Fritz Lang's "M",
half a mile away
Jackie stepped off a well-lit bus
onto a well-lit, shop-lined street
in her flat comfortable shoes
and her sensible coat, collar up
to keep her safe from a November wind
and because her long, dark skirt had twisted
on the bristly seats of the number 56

.../..

she turned to straighten it,
and then she walked straight home
followed by a man with a pocket full of screwdrivers.

117. Voodoo
LINDA ROSE PARKES

She takes her anorak from the cupboard
on a rainy morning; that afternoon
still clinging to the fabric however
many times it is washed and spun.
Two boys from her class calling her *tart,*
throwing her satchel in the mud.

The moment they spit on her coat,
does she realise what it is they want to
exorcise, what they cannot name or touch?
Her conical breasts, rounded thighs,
rough–gold pubis.
The twin demons of desire, self–disgust.

118. For Women
CAROLE LUKE

The silent army of angry men
move quietly forward to their prey.
Charming, behaving impeccably,
Soft spells they weave with silken play
entrapping hearts in manicured hands,
Carefully wrecking, but quite respectably.

Revenge the call for hurts they feel
Disguised with words spun fine.
To hurt, retaliate and pierce
The soft, sweet shell of those
who cared.
The soft sweet shell of those
who dared
Love the men so dear but fierce.
the silent army of angry men.

119. The Lard Man
TERESA MIDDLETON

I opened the front door.
The Lard Man.
Grey–white face – waxy.
Dirty white.
Unhealthy. Sinister.

His mouth was opening and closing,
Like a guppy.
I smiled.
Turned up the heat.
And he started to run.
Dripping.

Later I went out.
And wiped the fatty smears
with some kitchen roll.

120. Mick The Bouncer
LILLY JACKSON

He's got no neck just head and shoulder
Says he's thirty looks much older
Drives an Escort Cabriolet
In ghastly stripes of pink and grey
In the summer there he is
Strutting like he is god's gift
He pumps iron can't you tell
Does a few steroids as well
He has a Rottweiler called Tyson
Which has the body of a bison
There they go down the street
To the gym where bouncers meet
Mirror Mirror on the wall
Who's the toughest of them all
Tonight I expect we'll all find out
Coz in the club with chest puffed out
You'll see him there he's Mick the Bouncer
Known to all his friends as Pouncer.

121. Feminist–Phobia
NAOMI HUTCHINGS

The other day I read
About a group
For men who felt threatened by feminism.
Perhaps, I thought,
Walking home late at night,
Under the streetlamps
Through each pool of light,
Watching for shadows,
Listening for footsteps,
They imagined an attack by a feminist.
Or, perhaps,
One summer afternoon,
Minding their own business,
A group of feminists on a building site
Asked them for sexual intercourse.

122. Women's Lib
HELENE M. GARVIE

You said "Yes", you said "Yes"
I nearly fell off my chair
and then it sank in – You'd said "Yes"
Oh God! How had I dared?

I started to panic, got into a flap
and then tried to put you off
giving you all sorts of excuses to let you back out
or to tell me to get stuffed

But you said "Yes", you said "Yes"
you'll go on a date with me
I've asked you now and you said "Yes"
so I guess we'll just wait and see!

123. Brief Encounter
KATE COPPENHALL

A brief encounter
between two poets,
talking through the night
while the sky becomes a grey light
through the attic window.
Only stopping when the birds
wake the city streets and
the buses start to hum.

She, in awe of his scholarship and words,
wonders what he learned from her, of her,
in an encounter as familiar as time:
male ego attendant woman.

124. Roger McGough
POLLY HEYES

It's Roger McGough
Again,
I see.

The usual voice,
On FM
And TV.

It's Roger McGough,
I see,
Again.

The popular choice,
Maybe.
But then,

It's Roger McGough,
Again.

125. Sucking On Shells
TANIA CASSELLE

You're the same as Everyman
but you wear a better brand of face
and seem to understand the codes
a woman has tattooed beneath her skin.

You sport your intuition
like a pink carnation in your buttonhole,
and images of moons
and mother seas
and nurturing breasts
float beautifully
upon your silvery speech
and trick me into thinking
you have crossed the river
to the soft green lands
where women sit in circles
cradling mystery in their laps.

You wear our colours well,
sit barefoot in our light
and sing our rhythms
quite convincingly.

But sorry.
Till you've swum beneath a man,
absorbed him in your fullness,
till you've looked into your mother's eyes
and seen your replica reflected back,
then all you have to suck on is a shell.

Return it to the beach for tides to fill,
and go,
go blow your horn.

126. New Man, New Euphemism
LOULOU BROWN

He says: "Shall we make breakfast?"

He says: "Shall we buy the food?"

He says: "Shall we decorate?"

He says: "Shall we clean the house?"

He says: "Shall we eat now?"

He says: "Shall we mow the lawn?"

He says: "Shall we have a cup of tea?"

He says: "Shall we take the children
            to stay with your mother?"

He says: "Shall we go away, on holiday?"

For "Shall we?" read "You fix it, partner".

127. Tube Pain
RACHEL WATSON

Annoying tone
Of mobile phone
Central Line
To Leytonstone.
I'M ON A TRAIN
I'M ON A TRAIN
CAN'T YOU HEAR?
I'M ON A TRAIN.
Man in a jacket
Makes a racket.
We all stare at
Old crisp packets.

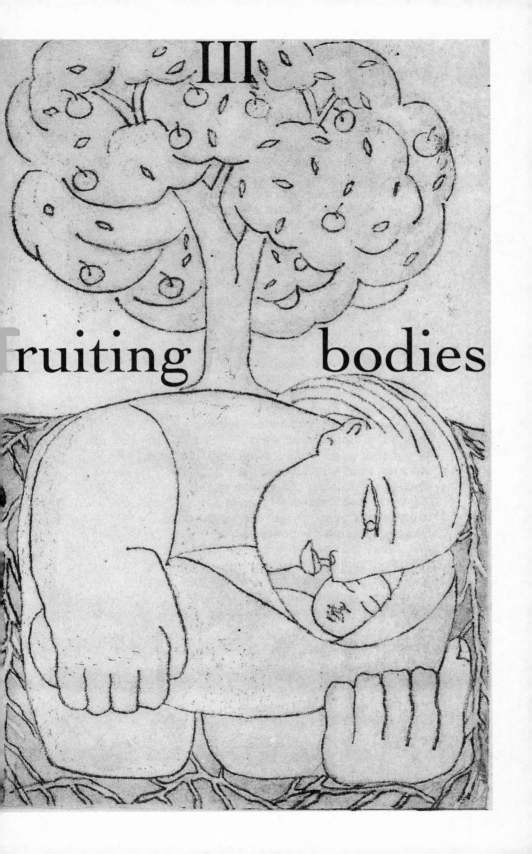

III

fruiting bodies

128. No Conception
SHEILA E. SMITH

You tumble into bed at night
To love your partner rotten.
You're both revved up and on the verge.
There's something you've forgotten.
To halt right now would kill the mood.
It's hardly the occasion
To calculate the timing
of a body's ovulation.
To sew the seed of babyhood
Could never be a sin.
Get on while passion's flying high
And prick the dibber in.
Don't dwell for half a second
On those nightly, howling scenes,
Or reflect on the resultant
Combination of your genes
That could recreate a schnozzle
To resemble Auntie May's,
Who would visit you twice weekly
Just to criticise your ways,
While that seed would swell and blossom
And its feet would elongate
And your clothing bill would spiral
At some ever-soaring rate
Till Junior's prey on earth's resources
Seem too great to contemplate!
Your partner has gone quiet
And you look down in dismay.
You slump sideways on a whispered sigh,
"We'll try another day."

129. Extra Time
KATH McKAY

The terrain is different now. No signposts.
A different ballgame if you want to be funny
On this post-vasectomy field.
Cod-piece hung up to dry like a one breasted bra,
Small line of bumps across your balls,
Stitches gathered together
Tiny threads dissolve in the baths you oh so gingerly take
Containers labelled 'semen' wait to be filled
In three months' time.

'You're my last baby', you say to our daughter,
as you snuggle down to read,
her wide-cheekboned face next to yours.
'Don't die', you say, a catch in your throat,
'I'll try not to', she laughs.
The slow crab of regret crawls over the house.
Never, it says, never, never again.
Old age and emptiness.
Pitch bare.

It's midsummer, next door shouts fly through open windows,
as Ireland lose to Mexico,
they have the barbecue anyway,
smoke curls before the storm sending lightning shivers
across the park.
Children throw basketballs high in the air
the scent of honeysuckle wafts across, it's mixed with dog.

Glastonbury; we watch on late TV, and sweat,
Somewhere inside a memory's loosed,
and lust comes unannounced, like after childbirth,
we're in our bodies like no other time;
Slow falling into each other's arms,
Slow suck of flesh on flesh, no barriers.
We know now why your balls were tweaked and pulled.

And part of me can't believe
we're entitled to this.

130. The Planting Of A Seed
RHIANNON FOX

Such a natural need
With a bitter taste,
It makes her heart bleed,
She feels disgraced,
Accused of greed,
With fear she has faced,
The planting of a seed –
Clinically placed.

Such a natural need,
But she must make haste
Unlimited is the speed,
Of time and space.
And no–one can believe
The sorrow she has faced,
The planting of a seed –
Clinically placed.

Such a natural need,
And without a trace
of selfish greed,
It is genuinely laced
With a love that is freed
From a barren waste.
The planting of a seed –
Clinically placed.

131. Office (Feb. 1979)
JEZEBEL

Grey Day.
Tall, north–shaded room.
Harbinger of others' fears,
        mistle–thrush and grinding gears.
Typewriter, talk, and silent tears.
Frozen embryo in eternal tube.

132. In Vitro
GINA RILEY

You come to light
before your time, conceptions
of you clinical, if cradled in clear glass.
A shaft of green . . .
all that it implies – aside from Eden's
brand of apple – sandpies on a beach
school swimming galas, birthday jelly
and bouncy castles. A fixed address
as crazy as the Land of Oz
when wizardry is foreshadowed
by the deft man–ipulation
          of a lab technician's glove.

Your mother leaves you
before you come to life, steps back
to wait and will you
to succeed. Now you can
be lifted up . . . catch the sun! before inheriting
earth and heaven, revolve around
the IQ of an embryologist's eye, window
blinds open to wider airstreams, microscopic
forms of life
          even if you happen to die
          before you begin to live. You surely

come to life
as the vital point of a further issue
the right to choose
or not. A reality
where gold slides and a rosepink ribbon
are not always leading strings

only part of an Adventure Playground
beyond all childish dreams.

133. Mirror, Mirror
FIONA CURNOW

In a silvery place
I have drunk from the breast of the full moon mother
To feed the empty place of motherness in me.

Wives grow creases
In the corners of their eyes
To channel tears discreetly to the pillow.

And I have cried wife-tears
In silence
As if unlovely women need less loving.

But in a silvery place
The full moon mother's tears
Are white, like milk.

134. Under Neon
FIONA CURNOW

I cannot see the moon.
Street lamps too ugly bright,
The untrained water in me has no tide to tell it why.

I cannot see the moon:
I don't know when to plant
What should be planted when white lady rises.

I cannot see the moon
And menstruate without example,
Chaotic and unfruitful like the wind.

Moonstruck lunatic madwoman howling for the moon
I cannot see. An angry orange citiglow
Is smothering the night.

135. Gardening
FOKKINA McDONNELL

I tried growing cabbages,
but they got eaten
by the slugs.
So it's back to the clinic –
further tests,
more drugs.

If I had my time again,
they say,
I would not have kids.
I probably would not
want to have them either,
if I could.

136. Smudge Baby
ANNE RYLAND

In my wandering fantasies
I have struggled to keep
your wriggling shadow
close to my stone womb.
I think you were watching me
as I engraved
endless trusting dreams there
within the honoured grave
of my belly,
but now the waiting ceremony
is fading and I hear
your Goodbye footprints
slipping away beyond
the bare years ahead.
The bruise of emptiness is
closing round;
now we will never paint
our life together.

137. Just In A Dream
LYNDA MARK

She speaks to me as blissful slumber dreams
To tell of a child I never knew
snatched before a moment's love
no grieving time for her
Now here she sits with my little ones
mingling as if to belong
Older than my firstborn, just as it would have been
And although her form eludes me
I know that she is mine until the morning breaks
when the warmth of her embrace
will fade into that time for sleep
Lost to me in a moment
so silent is my grief!

138. To my daughter Alice, who died suddenly and unexpectedly at 8½ womb months
KATE GILLIE

As my own mother, unwilling, let go her breath
having tried to contain me
her lips pressed together until blue
her cheeks bursting
her thighs aching to close
full two months early
I was born, in a sudden bloody slurry
caught by the foot, it is said,
thanks to a canny midwife's quick wrist

At birth I was the size of one of my father's fists
Strange, then, that you were worth
at least three of mine
You enjoyed the warm, watery world
of your mother's comfort
longer than I
and yet I lived
and you did not
Did my blood grow tired
of pumping an everlasting repetition
around both our bodies,
did a chink grow somewhere
like a tumour would, unknown, a
kink in the cord of love that flowed from me to you
Or did a chain of circumstance
holding a false
a hidden link
undo
all that had been done

with   such love
            such certainty

139. Absent
BARBARA COURTENAY

I would
write short letters
just to be heard by them
as they found it difficult to
listen.

Mother
shuts her eyes tight
turning her head away
and making impatient noises with
her mouth.

Phone calls
non-stop chatter
of grandchildren and food,
shopping and cleaning, with no pause
for thought.

Other
people's babies
are all she talked about
choosing not to mention the loss
of mine.

140. Right of Passage
DIANA SYDER

You all talk easily of births
as if they were some sloppy
throw away beauty
you have the keeping of.
You say your most intimate words
in unison and I examine the floor
not to see your pride
and to let this sharpest absence
roll from my shoulders,
settle sore at my front.

I am no child.
I am no mother.
But I stand
and with all your women's talk
you will not dissolve me
along the length of your shores.
The rush of your collective birthing
cannot smash my vast caves.
Rather I would show you out
and ask you not to come here anymore.

141. Dead Babies
JACQUELINE FERREIRA

Dead babies tell no lies.
No, just the truth.
Lingering bloody evidence
Of love gone wrong.
Or love that never was.

Hollow pain whose throb
Salts other wounds.
What might have been
Bleeds enough, let alone,
Who might have been.

142. The House On Fire
(Conversation after a Cot Death
– for my Daughter)
ISABEL GILLARD

"You drew this picture, bright with coloured chalks,
its message such as any mother makes
for reassurance and with love,
'Here are the walls, the rosy sheltering roof, the
door we use to venture out,' it says.

"The windows, evenly set on either side,
look on the lawn, where only yesterday
we gathered crimson apples, fallen too soon
after this generous summer sun.

"No doubt you'd have gone on to draw the tree,
explained the apple–fall,
had not your daughter snatched the brightest chalks
and drawn her infant swirls over the half–built house
– a hieroglyphic tale too difficult to read.

"No–one will know now if her little hand
confirmed the structure of the house you drew
or gave her own great version of the truth.

"Looking from here, it seems as if the house
blazes with kindly fire, rained from above,
the walls expanding in such radiance,
its little shelter needless
in the great sun's warmth."

143. To A First Grandson
PHYLLIS HILL

Small, Celtic eskimo in pastel wool,
exploring a private sky
with clutching, groping hands,
and thrusting your wild, ecstatic limbs against
my warm, resistant palms,
you did not know the joy,
the love that heralded your birth
woke fading, plaintive echoes
in my heart.

You could not know one distant yesterday
there came another you –
another child, all mine –
with eyes that followed, followed, just as yours,
and same lop–sided smile.
Twelve loving weeks he stayed –
my son, my only son
snuggled against my breast
and then – was gone.

Dear, Celtic eskimo in pastel wool,
still lying open–eyed,
forgive, and understand
the deep, unnatural silence when we met
was Time that had to be;
in that ungracious pause
a small, persistent ghost
was being laid, to free
my arms for you.

144. Pregnancy Blues
CHRISTINE PAICE

When I sit in my lair
like a bad tempered camel
trying to knock the zoo keeper's hat off,
I am surprised by the wisdom of the zoo
keeper.
Instead of ducking and diving and
pushing me away,
he gives me his hat to eat.

gnash gnash my teeth
oil my belly
think boy or girl?
chew hat.

145. On Giving Birth
CHRISTINE KITSON

And God created Man
And Man created stirrups
And who said that
Giving birth was beautiful
With your legs trussed
Up in the air
Like a chicken
With one major difference
The stuffing's coming out . . .

146. First Sight
PATRICIA BERYL BECKWITH

There they were, face to face, for the first time.
Seemed funny meeting like this: their relationship
began some months before. They had often communicated
each in their own special way. They had shared the same
space. But now, after this labour of love, their eyes met.
A moment of recognition. "So that is what you look like."

147. For David, New-Born
CHRIS HACKETT

How to begin? How
even to see you through tears? To welcome
in trembling cheers the smallest wonder
the massive fact
of your life.

The fierce release:
the hallowed landing
of your birth.

The top of your head: velvet
borrowed from petals.
Your skin's breath
as softly given.

Little limbs pedalling furiously
the tiny bike you must have ridden
in heaven.

Shrill cry that breaks
to a melting chime.
Stunned eyes searching, searching:
resting on mine.

May they never
limit your view, little seer!
Never limit your view.

148. New
DENISE McSHEEHY

Surprisingly solid
and red
as if you're overdone
or peeled

papery scales
still sticking
to fingers
and toes

hair greased
to your skull
a gummy whine
mine?

These scrawny legs and arms
make me think
of wishbones
will they snap?

I like it best when
folded in a shawl
you focus
attention
like a small saint

everyone
wants to hold you

I'm someone else
heady with tiredness
tuned to you

the way you sink
into yourself
propped up for a burp
head bobbing

the frail stem of your neck

149. In The TV Lounge
JAN NATANSON

Here we lurk, hiding
from mewling newborns
and the slender waists
of bossy midwives.
Jellyfish, with trailing
seaweed hair and
prawn pink faces.
Our quilted nylon puffballs
are in various stages
of deflation.
Some perch on chairs
as if on the edges
of razor shells.
Others loll like sacks;
flotsam with corpse white
blue veined legs.
We flick ash and glance
at the door with defiant eyes.
A last rebellion
against maternal duty.
We are tangle, washed up
along the telly's shore.
The rippling tide of
shared chocolate has
receded. Left us stranded.
We do not talk.
We watch the screen.
Hear our past lives
echo in a conch shell
held up to our ears.

150. The Welcoming Party
HEIDI JAMES

These are the spires our
penniless boredom reaches
here is our configuration of sleep
it is a bed
this is our kitchen, scribbles of crumbs
left over, our own sacred pollution
here is our bookcase a little heavy
with tomes abducted under our coats
that is our rug brittle with remnants
from the streets
these our photos, old skins outgrown
pickled on paper
that is a candlestick preserved
for power cuts, a famine in the meter
and romance
He is your God your Maker and Taker
this is me and i
am your mother.

151. Dream Day
MOIRA CLARK

In the dawn we sleepily greet each other,
your tiny hands unfurling
like leaves rejoicing in the sunshine.

As the sun rises, you paint our world
with warmth and innocence,
enriching the greys with colour.

At noon there are no shadows,
so we play with reality
and discover new meanings.

As the sun wanders wearily away,
we cling to each other in the twilight
and dream of another day's beginning.

152. My Son
CHRISTINE CURRY

Round, brown and gentle
my son sits on the sand
solitary in his thoughts of childhood.
Could I conjure
would I keep him
forever in innocence
or would I wait
and slowly watch
my love grow to a man.

153. Jessica's Birthday
SUSAN PARTINGTON

Today, my daughter unwraps another year,
Excitedly tears layers from the present,
Glimpses future pleasures,
Proudly three.
Content with balloons, games and party tea,
Busy-ness stops for traffic-light red jelly.
A camera records the candles' extinction
In a flash
Containing us all within its frame,
Recording forever, the present,
Grandma's jumper, knitted (too big) with memories,
Unseen, the umbilical cord
No birthday can sever.

154. She tells him about gravestones
ROSALEEN CROGHAN

On our way to the hospital, we passed through
the bald and mossy slopes of the churchyard of St. Giles.
And after he had threaded them in and out,
I told him that the gravestones would mark the place
where we were buried when we had died,
when we had all died and they had buried us.
Hand in hand as we walked through I felt his warmth
and the blood race sweetly beneath his sticky palm.

155. Nine Years
ANNA MERYT

Childhood has flown
I tried to make every moment
Precious and lasting.
But my hand reaching out
To grasp it, hold it
Has felt it turn to quicksilver
And slip through my fingers
Insubstantial as air.
Now in sadness
And resignation
I watch your last year
Of childhood
Slip quietly past
And mourn.

156. Feelings
ANGELA GREENHILL

"My feelings hurt!" you said, and crossed your arms.
  Crimson-faced you stomped off down the hall
  To sit alone, incensed, beyond recall,
Eyes full of tears. No blandishments or charms

Could win you back. In every inch of you
  Sharp anger crackled. What the hidden cause
  Or how we'd broken your unwritten laws
I'm not quite sure – perhaps we never knew.

How did we heal at last that burning sore?
  I think old Rupert Bear, a trusted friend,
  Edged round the door, pleading that war should end.
You smiled, reluctantly. You were just four!

And so to bed. "Sleep tight, my love, sleep tight,"
We said, and anger vanished in the night.

157. Freya Blows
CHRISTINE PAICE

Her sweet breath crickles
over the flame
Freya's life will never
be the same
now she knows
how to blow
the match out.

With eyes as wide
as a hippo's side
and as round and clear
as a great white moon
Freya laughs and blows
Her joy so pure
Only my love
can match it.

158. Tending
GILL HORITZ

Gardening in the undergrowth
of hydrangeas. I rake and rake
with pleasure in the tug of autumn's haul.

One scalp I raked that way
with wordless shuttling of hands
and tender fettling at start of day:
stooped over my daughter's head
to make a fine white parting
between six thick hanks.

Now I tend bushes, till borders
and think of my girl, plaitless
in the streets of Budapest,
whose hair I once coiled
into golden stooks.

159. Celebration
MARISHA ROSE

Morning
I brush my daughter's hair
Stroke it smooth
Cross each tress over to form a tidy plait.
Wisps of hair touch her face.
Turning, she leaves the room
And the plait free follows.
I watch her leave for school,
Switch the radio on
To kill this breathing silence.
Pick up the strewn toys
The room looks empty now;
Bigger, colder.
I decide to bake bread
Harvest festival soon.
I carry the warmed bowl against my stomach
Heavy but empty.
Fill it quick
Flour, salt, milk and yeast.
Kneaded, proved, risen.
I carefully take dough from the bowl.
Clinging desperately it tears from the sides.
I reshape this mass into snake like strips
That thrash their tails when I press and roll,
Plait my bread and glaze with egg.
Put into the oven until the pinger alerts me.
This golden bread.
Mine to give.

160. Domestic TeDeum
MORAG HOLDEN

Kids are
such agenda benders, chopping away
at coherence.
Amidst the debris of family life
keeping entropy at bay
is my current preoccupation,
gathering up scattered thought processes
while I meditate on the transmigration of socks

The universe beckons, its black holes
filled with coathangers, biros
and lost marbles
(maternal)

161. Motherhood Too
MARY JAY

The cries woke me.
Stepping on cold lino, I picked the baby up.
Wet both ends and yelling for food.
The day had started.

The others soon joined us.
Amid chaos, squabbles and TVa.m.
Breakfast was made and eaten,
Uniforms ironed and put on.

Swift movements through crowds
Huddled together under umbrellas,
School first, shopping next, washing later.
Brain, dulled by monotony, numb.

Tea over, kids in bed,
Too exhausted for anything but sleep
I climbed the stairs, hoping that tonight
Teething pains would take a break.

At least in prison
There's time off for good behaviour . . .

162. Whoops!
TRACY ELLIS

I'm going to mass at 11 o'clock
My daughter myself
and three little tots.

The Holy water's there
for me and you
and even for the man
that skidded to his pew

We kneel to Jesus
and take our seat
The lady in front
finds my baby at her feet

They climb over and under
and round and through
God loves little children
don't you just too!

I have bread and wine
and go into retreat
and then with loudest voices
they shout for a sweet.

Mass is over
I leave for home
Oh I've left them there!
I've come home alone
Whoops!

163. Monoprinting
ANN WHALLEY

Side by side we work,
engrossed,
putting colour on colour,
shape on shape,
happy to be creating.
But what changes the years have brought.
Less tentative now,
we create subtler, fuller designs.
You've blossomed
and now help me to grow
as once I showed you the way.

164. Lovechild
JOAN HAMMERTON

This Godlike
Bacchus child,
Child of the grape
Like wine
Goes to my head
And heart
The cockles warming:
Sweetly intoxicates
My senses
Until my cup
Of happiness
Runs over
With the loving.
This fiery Spirit
Ferments, explodes
With righteous indignation –
Then settles,
A rare vintage,
A veritable flagon
Of sweet juices
To mellow
My old age.

165. The Son's Room
BRIGHID SCHROER

I close the door to your room.
I know enough now.
I've seen the snot like gum,
Read the obscenities.

The walls are streaked with brown
Where your posters burned.
Charred strips hang down
With finger smears.

The window netting's torn
Where you climbed in.
We've nailed the frame down.
The afternoon sun

Shines between pasted panes
Across curled papers,
Cups, tapes, earphones
Junked on your desk

To the black—ink stain on the floor,
Split shoes, clothes, a bowl
Stuck with cereal, a jar
Growing soft mould.

The boombox is broken, the mattress
Slit with a knife. Fifteen
And away, you've left ashes,
Cupped foil in a box.

You shadow me ankle to shoulder
When I turn my head
From the morning paper
With its photos of riots,
Reports of the dead.

166. Times Two
MOLLY MAUGHAN

One two is two
Two twos are . . .
Four pence don't make a phone call.
Three twos are . . .
Six pence short in her purse.
Two months
He'd been given;
Four twos are
Eight weeks inside
Over Christmas, New Year
Leaves her and three children
Two visits,
Two letters
Tuesday's okay
Family Allowance day.
Saturday's okay
Giro day . . .
It's Thursday today
No money day.
'Can you give me six pence
Please' – she asked a stranger,
'I need to ring school.
They'll keep my three children
Till I say my goodbyes.
He's going at two
He's going to . . . '
She whispered . . .
'I can't say the word.'

167. Separation
CARO LEE

The sting of pain as little
Loving hands are wrenched
From me as they cling
In a dark London street
Damp with wet and cold
And my heaving chest
Holding back sobs that
Wrack generations of mother love
And fighting women.

Years later because you knew
I loved you, you come
Rushing, laughing, dancing
Into my childless life.
Father to the mother now
Huge arms surround me
In warm protection, at last
Refreshed I rest my heart
And the earth smiles briefly
And so do I.

168. The Flesh House
HELENA HINN

I sew the Flesh House
– hem it together
I take the uneven fabrics of joy, pain and indifference
and stitch them together
I am the mother of the home
its nuclear heart

my welding love is muttered low, on a hostile night
to a pensive child
my soft breast a harbour
my whisper a reassurance

I sew up discords
and I mend hearts

169. Special Daughter
ANNE BERRY

I did for her what I would not do for my own.
Her day was always special.
We all did whatever she wanted to do.
We walked, rode and cycled with her.
Every minute was precious.

We always saved her every surprise,
and tried to make her day different.
Dietary requirements were always observed,
her friends were always welcomed.
There were parties and presents and lots of fun.

Now she comes no more,
It was her choice to leave us and never return.
We have to live without her
I am not a wicked queen or an old witch.
I can never be a 'step' again.

170. Enigma
JEAN MITCHELL

Special wavelengths for this special child,
    elusive as Peter Pan, avoiding capture
    by maturity. The focus shifts . . .
Does he know that I am here, or who I am –
    for he avoids the human eye   –
    or is it just coincidence?

It seems fear has made speech her home,
    so how express with minimal talk
    is now the question.
Whether any form of communication
    would be acceptable to the recipient
    is a matter of conjecture.
The great teachers, having failed to evoke,
    to date, a perfect guarantee
    that thoughts put out upon the ether
Will be picked up, the question
    must remain: to write, to mime,
    to sing? But not to speak,
A message of love to an empty face.

171. To A Son, Short On Chromosomes
WENDY HOLT

Under the earth the esoteric crystals
Obscurely flash their arcane code,
Delivering an unspoken utterance
Like the silence of sun on snow.

God has prevented this world,
Laid traps.
Transfixed by clues, the crystal gazers
Grope on the charnel floor,
Raking the ashes.

Stand up, son, you are for demonstration,
A secret message carrier:
You are ripe for the dissecting knife,
Singled out.

You may not sit idly fishing by the river,
Dart your keen canoe over the falls,
Scuff your shoes in the park.
You can take nothing for granted
Except that I will not allow *my* son
To be pinned on a Cross.

For here the Almighty hiccuped, threw the switch,
Covering his tracks with a crafty re-set
Of co-ordinates, changing the combination
To fox a cracksman.

Unbaffled, my special boy,
We will defeat his object.
Innumerate,
We need only ignore the evidence
And accept your half-truth
To make a fool of God.

172. Taboo
ASTRA

my sons and i
can't grow
to know
each other's flesh

it has been done
by some
though no one
tells

it turns me on
to think of it
my sons and i:
our flesh
one flesh

we know each other's bodies now
from outside in and inside out
we really know
but no
we mustn't show
or tell

here we are
shedding clothes
showing limbs backs hair
shedding layers
stroking hair limbs backs
shedding limits
smoothing backs hair limbs
shedding
stroking
shedding
smoothing

showing

telling

173. Tulips
MURIEL GRAINGER

These prim and tidy tulips,
Tight shut around their secret selves,
Stand like red-coated soldiers
In their transparent vase,
Each one a mirror-image of the rest –
A repetition of a perfect form.

I would rather have a children's bunch of daisies,
A honeysuckle-tangle; one red rose.
Somehow their uniformity
Conveys the feeling that they preen themselves,
Sharing a sense of strange self-satisfaction.

174. Tulips
CLARE DRUCE

What if the passion of the flowers
should mock his dull deceit?
I arrange them lovingly,
one by one.

Crow-purple,
sun-gold,
licking tongues of flame.
Gradually,
they tell their secrets.

From depths of darkened intimacy,
black powdered stamens
lie exposed.
Finally,
voluptuously,
the dying tulips arch their petals,
in ecstasy.

175. Blackthorn
CLARE DRUCE

Someone brought in a branch of blackthorn,
flowering,
broken from the hedgerow,

I stood it in a vase.
Needing no arranging, it spread out,
perfect,
in starry splendour.
Happiness took me by surprise
and stayed with me all day.

176. Plane Trees
LYNDA HOLLAND

A breeze stirs the fetid air
Pollution lies heavy on you.
Leaves caress the fitful breeze
Playfully tickling the air.

A grey, damp day in London Town
Your restless home.
Stately presences,
You embrace us fondly.

177. Sunflowers
HEATHER WOOLLEY

Sunflowers in September
Glory faded
Yellow-green and wilting
Heads drooping
Darkened faces, fringed by light
A group of women, mob-capped
Mourning, weeping

178. Sarah
CLARE DRUCE

A tumbling hillside,
washed eye-blue with lowly speedwell,
mirrors the sky.
Furled leaves,
made reckless by spring sunshine,
break free of winter's dying grasp
to paint the wood,
rising from the deep-down stream,
with tracery of dazzle-green.

Pale cotton dress translucent,
the child stands
in the bright meadow.
Holding a posy close, she understands
the minute but staggering
perfection
of the sky-enamelled flowers.

179. Alchemilla Mollis –
St. Beuno's
MARY E. NONO

A neglected garden
treasure veiled
Mary's mantle, choking
with bindweed.

Not so-yew-strong,
haughty on hallowed ground,
pruned by path,
in woodland, wild and free.

You, Veronicas, stand and wave
terry-towelling tails, blue and lilac.

Silent bells in cottage hedgerow.
Chelsea cannot compete
with Coed Canterbury!

180. Welcome Callers
PAT ARROWSMITH

Pigeon arabesque,
Kinetic sculpture of frenetic wings –
Billowing yacht sails flapping flaglike
As they jostle, squabble,
On the seed-strewn table.

Or peace-doves they may squat
Drowsily meek under my cupped hand,
Lids slowly shuttering sleepy eyes,
Necks bowed,
Heads drooping down in semi-slumber.

Sometimes lively, playful,
Their beaks point up to be caressed,
Or strain to poke and rub between my fingers,
Gently pecking them
In cheeky pigeon greeting.

I am sixty-three,
Without partner, children, cat or dog;
So these regular dove visitors,
Unhouse-trained,
Noisily demanding though they be,
Are much loved welcome callers;
Have become quite special
And among my closest friends.

181. On The Tube
MARY WOOD

What must the other passengers have thought?
Was I, frail, eighty, solely the one who saw
The pigeon flutter through the open door
Of the tube-train? Were they never taught
To look?

Well out of place, but still at home, content,
It pecked precisely at the long-barred floor
Of the carriage. Nature and Man's graffiti never meant
To meet in here   –   and, seemingly, only for
My eyes.

So many years ago, I really can't recall,
Five of us took a trip to Drury Lane.
Four boys and I . . . the tube train home again . . .
Downing the escalator to the booking hall . . .
One bulging pocket . . .

I took it back, facing the stares and travellers' smiles . . .
Fluttering, struggling captive, held within one hand.
Feathers trail-telling pigeon and flushed anxious man
Traversed the downward movement upward miles
To light.

182. Communion
VIRGINIA ROUNDING

She's there most days –
seated on a mound above dilapidated roundabouts,
shuttered tea and coffee stalls, a line or two of washing,
the unchained dog rampaging in the drizzle.

She doesn't opt for picturesque surroundings –
most likely couldn't pull her shopping trolley further
or wants to know she's not too far from habitation
as, alone and mildly trembling, she feeds the birds.

They settle round her, peck across her shoulder,
treat her like a latter–day St Francis –
their wariness of other humans undiminished
by their trust in her –

if any come too near or loud they scatter,
chorus over caravans and puddles,
chagrined as she is to have their feast disturbed:
the giving and receiving of the bread.

183. The Bats
SALLY ST.CLAIR

  night–time   summer–time
the bats return at dusk
        black fairies
each a shadow of the other
    weaving together
        some mystery
  in silent frantic flight

184. Fox
SUSAN MAYER

I saw a fox today
trapped in a whitened garden,
a shock of orange skittering between dark boles of trees,
vivid as flame, darting at the fence.
And I, trapped behind glass,
watched him beat the bounds for his escape,
pitting the frost with prints of panic,
until with flattened arrow head
he stooped to brush beneath the hedge,
was gone – was free, alien intruder
from my suburban garden.

185. Fox On The Hill
TINKER MATHER

I am the fox at my feet

paws crossed when death
tripped her up in the afternoon

rust red blood
ears black as pen nibs pitched
to write

one eye open on
a herd of sheep

pink dyed ruffs blurring
with the wind

blown clean the feather dusters
of their minds

they pass over my flank

ruffling it a little with
their innocence.

186. Haiku
SUE LARKIN

Head lifted – dry bark
Wily, alert in cold dawn
Untamed urban fox.

187. Haiku
SUE LARKIN

Slaughtered pheasants
Sight of earthworks and carnage
Death by the red fox.

188. Lost Cat
DEBORAH SCOTT

We've lost the cat,
She has been buried with Beauvoir.
Will I ever find her again?

I think not.

Paranoid and terrified,
An overworked juggler.
Knowing something has to give.

What goes up Baby.

Chop off my head, I think too much.
And leave me dancing,
like a Headless Chicken
on a hot tin roof.

189. We Have A Cat
PHILIPPA DRAKEFORD

We have a cat,
And his name is Boz,
He looks with his eyes,
And he shniffs with his shnozz.
He eats like a dog,
And he trots like a yak;
He's really not good
At being a cat.

He butts his head
Against lots of things,
And sticks his bottom in the air,
When they handed out brains to Bozzy,
They really weren't very fair.
His round blue eyes,
Are always confused;
He's not quite sure
How his paws should be used.
He sharpens his claws,
On the carpets, chairs and door,
Flops on his side,
And stretches out on the floor.

But to make up for that,
he's a beautiful cat:
Chocolate point Siamese,
He has such lovely cuddly fur,
(It's a shame about the fleas.)
He's also very affectionate,
He'll rub round you and purr.
He'll curl up happy on your lap,
And moult off all his fur.

We have a cat,
And his name is Boz,
He looks with his eyes,
And he shniffs with his shnozz.
We have a cat,
And his name is Boz,
He's the funniest cat,
that ever was.

190. Snake
ELLEN ROSE BARTLETT

From the beginning snake came in dreams
Slow, thick bodied and deadly as congealing blood
With cold, cold cats eyes, or quick, quicker
Than fear, faster than thought, fangs fastened
In the neck before the eye understood movement
Or seething between the exposed joists of the attic
By the score, small as elvers, sinuous and fine
But impossible to pass.

With time snake slid into the eye of day,
The adder in the brambles, the asp in the storm drain
Heard before seen, scales rasping over dead olive leaves,
The slowworm sleeping in the warm ash of a field fire
And that big grey viper under the cherry tree
By the old well, where the madonna lilies nod
Keep away, keep away; and the signs of snake,
Leather eggshells in a drawer, flattened grass
Patterned by the bacchic knots of an undulating
April mating in the field of irises, and a shed skin
Brittle but complete.

And at last in a time of change and transmutation
I met with snake. Pure muscle poured round
My wrist and up my arm, dry, smooth and cool
Eyes still and steady, tongue quick as flame
And lay with its own due weight held firm
Across my shoulders like a friend. And there,
With all the little children, at the zoo, I knew snake
And smiled, and was disarmed.

191. I'm Not Afraid Of Spiders
JUDI BULL

I'm not afraid of spiders anymore
I can tolerate them on the bathroom floor.
I don't find it such a laugh
When they want to share my bath,
If it's sharing I'm to do
Then I'd rather share with you
With no more legs than two
And certainly not eight
So the spider meets his fate,
But I'm not afraid of spiders any more.

192. Lion
ROSIE GARLAND

Curls fall over its eyes.
It cannot walk but with an air of ownership.
It sways like a funeral cortege
and knows the grass will part before it.

It opens its jaws, leaking dead meat breath.
Voice loud and too familiar.
Its balls are huge, a brash advertisement
They swing uselessly against its thigh.

It watches the open moving mouths
of the surrounding creatures
and believes itself the root
of their wonder, worship and conversation
It cannot see they are yawning.

Far away across the plain
smaller, faster animals catch prey.

193. Ducks
NAWAL GADALLA

I remembered today the
joy you have in seeing ducks
and feeling with them
their intimacy and aptitude
oh their idiosyncrasies and their
quacktitude.

194. Of Swans And Angels
DORIS PALGRAVE

For weeks I've tried
to believe in angels
seeing them through sleepless nights
shaping their formations
struggling through my imagination
they turn into swans
sweeping down a silver pond
admiring their own reflections
intangible as small mountain clouds
floating away from outstretched hands.

Angels carry no reflections
remain as statues bleak and bare
have no substance, movement
nor cast any shadows.

I can believe in swans
their existence is there
as they stare down narcissi
drowned in that dark pool
where only the angels could live
if I could ever find them.

I must believe in angels
they are my protectors
watching patiently endlessly
as I float away with swans.

195.Oyster
JANE TARLO

Oyster asleep
Clings to its rock
Guards its pearl
Like a mother her child

The time has come
You will pluck me
From soft sea bed
An expert diver

Oyster is scared
Her mantle wrenched
By surgical hands
Into alien air

The time has come
Your hand will glide
Through green water
To reach me

A twist of the knife
So quick, so cold
Her child stolen
Oyster shrieks

Our time has come
I want you always
Beneath your shell
Soft as seaweed

Ashen alone
Oyster weeps
Shattered vigil
Now she keeps

The tide is coming
Walk with me
Over wild sand
And dream of pearls

196. Sandworms
ELIZABETH BIRCHALL

What runes in unknown hieroglyphs
Are written by worms
In the sand?

From damp, subterranean tunnels
They view our soles
Which crush their comments
On this world.

But when we've gone
They burrow and rise
And write again.

197. Beach
MARIE JAMES

The sand feels cold beneath my feet
Hard grains of life's experience
But the granules soften beneath my skin
As honied, sensuous waves roll in
Pushing pebbles of light between my toes
And a drowning spirit within me glows
Mulled by the warm, sagacious tide

But it ebbs as quickly as it flows
The pebbles of light between my toes
Are fossilised by ancient doubt
And they leave this wet and scuttling sand
Barnacled, drifting hand in hand
On a crest of insecurity

Sated seaweed nuzzle at my feet
Transferring their hue from the sea to the shore
Sapient starfish spread their arms out wide
Embracing the restless, rumbling tide

But all I can offer are footprints

198. Cormorant
EILEEN G. HARRISSON

Walking on beach
mirrored with rain,
wet sand;

footsteps dig deep
tide-pulled patterns weep,
bare sand.

Swish of cold sharp grass,
touch of skin wet hands,
wind blows;

cormorant swoops
black arrow to the flood,
tide flows.

199. Aldeburgh Morning
MAVIS DE MIERRE

Light strikes the chandelier of water,
A brilliant, prostrate beacon
Burning, fusing the nerve-ends;
The rind of lemon sun
Zests over the sea.
Brightness flares and prances,
Advances to invade the eye's lens;
Senses dissolve, dizzied,
Enticed, fractured.

200. The Sea
MOIRA HENDERSON

The soft curve of her woman surface
The rise and fall of her breathing,
My whole body longs
As I sit close beside her,
To be rocked in her arms forever.

201. Shore Walk
DORRIE MORRISON

In the mire of a deep depression
I sludged round the west shore.
All was grey
grey sky
grey sea
grey mist ridden rain.
I howled with the wind
raged with the sea and
cried with the gulls.

Then suddenly – quite suddenly
the mist cleared.
I watched the sun velveting
the sleeping mammoths of Hoy.
I saw the patchwork turtle back
of Graemsay rise out of the sea.

I sat on sun-warm rocks
my spirit swam with the seals
skimmed with cormorants
and paddled at the tide edge
with the Eiders.
The compassion of peace contented my soul.

202. Sunset Waterfall
DIANE PRITCHATT

An intoxicating mist
Touched the senses,
And I breathed
The breath of a frigid dragon
That roared
And sparkled his colours,
Splashing and clawing
In jewels
Over my submerged feet,
Burning and tingling the senses
Where fire and water fuse.

203. Rock (for Jen)
PAMELA COX

Rock solid, rock hard,
rock firm, rock safe,
rock sure, rock on until
the surface, worn, scratched,
broken down by wind, rain and frost
becomes particles of soft sand.

Together, they form a beach.
High tides buffet and separate them.
Shifting through fingers
they are buried and drown.
They are eaten, spat out,
stepped on, abused
and when the elemental rages subside
they glisten in the midday sun
like pins of pure gold.

204. Colour
DOROTHY SURTEES GOODMAN

Greyness descends
        The sky and the water merge
        The horizon is lost
The mist creeps out of the sea
        Shrouds the rocks
            the trees
A lost place
        A lost soul
The dripping of the trees
        blends with my tears

205. Icicles
ELIZABETH BIRCHALL

Too cold to sit
And study the delicate
Icicle in the rivulet.

Light and movement
Stopped in a translucent
Spire of water – instant

Impressions embroidered
By earlier remembered
Occasions, encountered

In childhood.
Hands stiff as wood
And chilled blood

But eyes fascinated
As fingers investigated
The columns congregated

Around the downspouts
Of our house.
Tasteless bite in numb mouth

And tough until
Touched; then merely chill
But, catching the sun, a miracle.

206. Angel Frost
JANET McDERMOTT

Angel's breath on a cold winter's night,
Tapping at the window, frost, fear and fright.
Cracked and chipped, the frozen glass of pain,
never to know well, only to walk in vain.
Feasting eyes upon an icicle nightmare,
white horses and legends once lived there.
Flying with the purpose of a dying breed,
with wings of fancy and a need to be free.
She's the lady in a white shroud of lace,
Forever watchful, eyes with no face.
She's a bitter moon, a harvest of snow,
a biting wind, the child of woe.

207. Candles
ALISON LAWSON

We should need more to
Create a universe. Yet
Tonight they burn, this very
Moment, a million small

Insignificances, to illumine
The gesture, far greater,
Hidden. Stars above,
Flames to reach out,

Kindled by air, by
Stillness. I gave you
One once, such a small
Gift, it burned steady

All night for you, for
Your father's journey,
Its extreme gesture
Of love.

208. After The Bonfire
LESLEY QUAYLE

It was
the last straw.

Flames incised the air,
talons running scarlet,
abased the timbers
and the rank stench of martyrs
trespassed my rooms.

The smoky musk
loitered idly round my head,
curling its breathy tendrils
through my hair,
like a lover's ghost.

Licking its slug black lips
the dragon retreats,
glutted,
smouldering,
reeking of nightmares.

It was
the last straw.

209. A Blue Glass
KIRSTEN LUCKINS

This was your gift to me

A blue glass like an upturned bell
A whirlpool held on a clear glass stem
This could hold everything
It has the time.

When children use their hands
To make flowers, they open like this
Like tulips, like bluebells
As if they could hold the light.

This was your gift to me

Solid liquid
Moving too slow for me to see
This has the time to settle
To hold the light and give it back to me

Altered, blue
And peaceful on my hands
Holding it.

210. 5,000 Miles From California
LISA RUDALL WORTHAM

This morning – missing home
First snow fell her face
Ice cut virgin fields, like
sun burns in a West Coast memory.
Last year Pacific waves curled her head.
Now, she paints home fading in borrowed colour.
Never before felt snow brush your face
Never before felt enchained in tender ice
Before, you walked gold in sunset sand
Now see an English winter chill you blue.

211. A Woman Stands
At Her Window, Late May
SALLY BAKER

Evening, and the rooms are light–filled
washed in sundown, and an outline
of trees dancing over hills.
She is holding out her hands, palm upwards

as though waiting to collect rainwater.
Rivers have run through her heart
and the leaves still on the branches.
She is speaking in grasses,

plantain and sorrel, marigolds drop
from her lips, face fevered from the day.
She is a shadow play, making tea
against the red wall, sun drowning in corn

watching the dot of a far off plane
move white across the falling sky
like an insect on her page, making
its way across whole alphabets, lines

of letters as though reading braille;
and the marks left by birds' wings
on her unsettled gaze, on that late heaven
crowded with the bones of angels.

212. Kew
AMANDA CORNU

The wind
blows and retreats
Leaves are tossed
Flutter downwards
Imperceptibly turn
Upon themselves
Whole trees shudder
Branches cracking
Leaves in turmoil
One's spirit is awakened
Excited by the fracas
Whilst the sun's rays
on this crisp autumn afternoon
pierce through
the flickering leaves
The beauty of these moments
poignant . . . everlasting
Greta and Chiquita interlaced
The one talks the other smiles
one ponders the other answers
both laugh
Happiness bubbling over
that cup of abundance
Perched on the Victorian glasshouse
My Patricia wheels on
Glances, falls in love
With a small pink flower
and dying red leaves
I stare and stare
At their blood redness
At their passionate ending
Oh, yes, to go out
burst forth
like a volcano
In such triumph!

213. Descending The Plateau
DIANE FAWCETT

Then we arrived.
Walking beneath those trees,
Past dense prickly heads, lilac and nettle.

Taunted by the four winds
Lilliputian we are;
Speckled by deciduous dazzlement,

Embraced, I quieten.
You hold my breath –
Stand where I can see you.

214. Dear Inspiration
SUE ORTON

Dear inspiration,

I had to get my DMs
before I went outside
for me
my feet are vital
to sense and touch the way
scrunchy gravel, sorting out, chilly inner thighs . . .
I tried to find you head down
Are you in a snowdrop bunched and snuggling?
muddy boots distract me,
I clean them on the moss and
contemplate the place of foot, each print,
despite the ache of wanting you to find me.

Damp, greenness, earth, squelching
trying too hard again.

215. Stone Walls
SARAH WHITEHEAD

Grey lines of pinched up
Plasticene at long distance,
Intricate close up.

Stone lines dribble down
Green & purple patch & brown
Patterns at Arncliffe.

Scrawled pencil lines on
Berghs & gills & fells & scars
Drawn down the valleys.

216. Bench
KATHRYN KNIGHT

It is nice to have
Somewhere nice to sit,
Isn't it! Doesn't
The wood look so good
Against the red sand
Wall, and thick ivy!
We could eat cake here,
Could eat home-made cake!
Could bring a good flask
Of hot red milkless
Tea, and be warm here!
The road's such a slope
A cobblestone slope
We can see right down
To the town centre!
And in the wall's curve
Have shelter! Shelter!
I'm thankful, dear love!

217. Sweet Pain
HEIDI FOSTER

Nature
proud
in its true unrelenting
beauty
intense, measuring
yet elusive
to the mind's need
to possess
with its painful
yet exhilarating simplicity
it overpowers
the sense of reality
and soothes
the turmoil within.

218. Country Banquet
GLEN SUMMERS

I watch as you run, pegs in mouth, to hang out
your washing,
Arms full of limp lettucey clothes,
You look like a demented sea-monster,
Red-armed and peg toothed you duck and dive
the kamikaze flies,
To open mouth would be to embrace their suicide,
Oh the joys of country life on this humid sticky wash-day,
The sweet fields are full of methane munchers and
shredded wheat bales,
Who's for three of these?
Crunch, crunch, munching in unison,
And the crust of flies around the eyes,
And the mossy messy midges in their beastly little swarms
Make ready their needles for one more blood red stab,
Did the scented honeysuckle entice you
outside to the banquet?

219. The Visit, Iona
MARY TAYLOR

She went to the Hill of Wine
to gather elderberries and broom
as he told her to in a dream
but fog, scrawling from Port of the Coward
blotted out woad and smudged her vision.
She found only hemlock and goblin apples
russet among thorns.
A peevish wind fretted and grumbled
withering her bittersweet bouquet
thrown to the lapwings' lochan.
Now she knows
        he will not visit again.

220. New Moon
TANIA CASSELLE

Such an impossibly thin shred of ivory
scratched in a fish-skin sky,
and the sun barely fled
from the horizon.

Sharp as a nail paring
hanging low in the two-tone dusk,
receptive to my gaze through the glass
she curls in a lazy smile of promise.
Her cup waits to be filled,
her belly to grow pregnant with light.

"Nothing but a dead planet," he said,
from behind me,
jealous at my wonder at another body
more powerfully curved than his.

Nothing but a dead planet.

So this is why the seas sing to her tune.

221. Storm Warning
HAZEL RENNIE

Yesterday, I rode with the Wind.
We dragged waves from the sea to the sky,
Flew upside down through a forest of trees
And when the Wind howled I shrieked in reply.
We chariot-raced the clouds round the hilltops
And round and round,
Drove headlong down the valleys
Rolling boulders of sound.
Then side by side, with powerful breast strokes,
We swam over the open heath,
Wind-surfing birds on our backs,
Sweeping the grasses beneath.
Then we hurled ourselves on the cities,
Whirling along shopping parades,
Beating the tower blocks punch drunk,
Flying paper flags up and down the arcades.
Lurking on corners like petty thieves
To rush and snatch at clothes and hair,
Whipping a furious frenzied rage
Before we sank on a last long moan of despair.
Yesterday, I rode with the Wind.
Today, the clouds of apathy remain
To blind and fog . . . and now I know,
Tomorrow, I must ride with the Wind again.

222. Searching for the Soul
RUTH STOTT

If I permit myself to be still
long enough
will I find myself
somewhere here in my head?

Or is my soul out there somewhere
awaiting the vigorous shouting
and windblown dancing
that will be my consummation?

223. View From The Steps Of The National Gallery
BARBARA M. STEWART

November sky, clear and pale
fading into rose madder pink,
Buildings silhouetted around the square,
Haze blurs the straining eyes
The sky is cloudless yet
there is a drift of smoke – a shadow
Long and sinuous whirling its way
into the night haunts of the City,
A rustling of a thousand starlings
Commuting to their nestling places.

224. Nothing Days
JOY FRASER

It's the grey days that are the life-stealers.
Not the crisp cold, brown gold days,
these are liveable with,
enjoyable to be in.
But the dank, bitter-berried
nothing days, they
cramp my stomach,
empty my mind,
and leave me winter bare in my soul.

225. Desolate
RUTH ATHRON

When you did not love me,
I went away down to the empty shore
And cried out my heart among the stones,
Where the grey water washes the stones:
But the waves echoed back my hurt to me,
Rising and breaking repeatedly.

226. April Showers
JOAN PLANT

Brave you are to follow March,
Him, with a belly full of wind
battering away at winter.

Soft you are, with misty eyes,
Always a hint of mischief as
you home in on summer.

Pale you are, clouded over
rinsed clean by your
silent showers.

Bonny you are, attention grabbing,
Flirting with nature,
Then comes the resurrection.

227. Love In Winter
MICHELLE MacGRATH

The waterlilly sings amid the snow.
The petals,
arms and legs entwined
and bound in loving,
float in fullness
slow,
so low and softly
quickening –
like voices chasing silence
fade and grow;
whilst all around
the six–point flower
falls,
and gently drifting,
flows
beyond pale birth
amid the snow.

228. New Year's Eve
GRETA ROSS

December'd skies berserk –
sun under siege as
night rapes light and
winds wild with winter
stalk and howl, mock
and rip the dying year

until
       the Old lets the New stroll in
       flush with resolves and auld lang synes,
       paymaster of memories,
       minder of myths and magical births,
and sly Old Nick sweeps the slates clean
and blues the skies with innocence

while
       implacably and silently
       seeds switch on,
       cycles begin,
       rhythms resume,
       and the Wheel of Life turns deep
       within earth and sea and bone.

229. By Altin Yuva
JANE TARLO

By Altin Yuva
Peeling grapes
I cupped sunlight
in my hands
swam in October blue
and ran
as day paled
path after path
hot, dusty
and a little lost
to find you.

Blossom floats
confetti
over water
this spring
peeling grapes
I drown in blue
having to stretch
my arms round
half the world
for just a rainbow chance
of holding you.

230. The Meaning Of Apples
LESLEY SAUNDERS

Soon the lawn will
be lush with rot,
the hard work
of making stop.
All flesh is infinitely
caressable, begs
to be thumbed and
mouthed and bruised
to sweet pulp before
it goes to the worms,

its haunches the colour
of claret, of amber, of
butterscotch and falling
every day a little more
in love with gravity,
pleading for one, only
one unbuttoned word or hungry
touch, promising
such exquisite memories.

Oh
and how you will be
punished, how
you will crawl!

231. Winter Love
JILL TRUMAN

When will you come, my winter love?
Frosty–hair and flaming loins,
To warm my chilly nights and
Blow with lusty breath the fog
From crannies in the long white days?

Quick – take my freckled hand
In your horny grasp and we'll stride
On sinewy legs up, up, up, into the hills:
And lie all day among heather and skylarks,
The sun on our cobwebby faces.

232. Harvest Honeymoon
VIV WACHENJE

Season of trysts and
Remembered fruitfulness,
When, in the midst
Of Devon's rugged beauty,
The innocence of Eden,
Already buried,
In favour and deferment
To the harvest of passion
And the sacrament of joy,
Became the communion of love.

Season of kisses and
Remembered completeness,
All in the end
Is harvest.

233. Idyll
ELEANOR ZONIK

From passion's flickering flame
Our late love came
And ecstasy was born
And all our world
Was torn apart.
But in the fire's heat
We found, coiled still and small
The pulse of peace, and we knew
All that love meant
In quiet content.
And now the air is gentle
Sliding into Spring.
Two herons pass
In an opal sky
Pale as old glass.
The stranded pools lie
Silver, where the grey tide ebbs,
And passion is re–born.
Tenuous as cobwebs
In an Autumn dawn.
Down in the bay
The sea's cold fingers brush
The shingle, whispering, hush!
The slow tide turns
And in the shouting silence
Our bodies meet, yearning and tense
And love we thought was past
Quivers and burns,
Sudden and secret
Like the flowering of the grass.

234. September
ROSEMARY HOGGETT

Summer's blood seeps
under nails,
purple–red dye
spreads on my hands.

Berries black, glistening
from early rain,
clustered in thorns
wait to be tasted.

This annual ritual
climbing the field
through long grass,
eye savouring

the distant hills
catching the first
glimpse of black–red hedgerows
brings tranquillity.

235. Alfresco (Tanka)
GILLIAN DENNISON

Black patent shoe–shined
rooks, shuffle fields, sileage shorn;
thick dibber beaks prod
summer's laden table top
drilling it a colander.

Unzipping the sky,
swallows, martins, swifts, picnic
high on scything wings
without tearing its blue cloth.
Summer living made easy.

236. The Seasons
IRENE LORCH

It is the winter scene that satisfies
because it tells the truth.

Spring says 'Come take my hand'
his firm young hand
and leads, the active hypocrite,
into green and buds and sap
'Look everything is new'.

Summer is a plutocrat
his greasy finger
points to opulence
of vegetables and flowers and fruit
'Enjoy my richness and my ripeness'.

Autumn droops a little
his ageing finger
wavers somewhat as he shows
trees and hedges beginning to decay
'Let my colours lull and soothe you'.

Winter does not need to advertise
arrogant, ascetic,
he strides his lands of desolation
through empty air and bitter skies
past leafless trees and frozen water
and hardened earth and tortured birds
through barrenness and nakedness
and purity and death.
'There is no mercy, everything must die.'

It is the winter scene that satisfies.

237. November 5th
JAN WHALEN

The leaves have left the trees
they are fallen mounds of whispering
skeletons curling and crumbling
into their own tiny hands.
It's a shame, you think,
the way the winter treats the trees
and the lake freezes over
and grows a skin to keep out the cold.

On Bonfire Night the pile of wood
is disturbed at last
and woken into roaring dancing
wild life
You have remembered the hedgehogs
and furry field mice
that might have been inside
you've told me again the legend about
Catherine and her wheel

and you find you are depressed
suddenly, inexplicably
in bed we hold on to each other
and wait for your misery to pass
Outside in showers of sparks
and the blazing heat of wood
the neighbours celebrate
the dead season with fireworks and fire.

238. Inscape
PAT BRISSENDEN

I accept the hidden designs
The exquisite touch of the pruner
And as the fullness of summer
Passes to mellow autumn
And life slows to a quieter winter
Your handiwork repairs and replenishes
And springtime heralds a new flowering.

239. Seasons
ERICA FEARN

You lay on scorched grass
And spoke with a sleepy, sun-filled voice.
Like honey on the comb, your words dripped sweetness
And your sky-wide smile was beautiful.

You looked out from the chill, grey room
And saw rain leaching colour from the fields.
Like a November sky, your face grew clouded
And the love leached out of your eyes.

I walked down the iron-cold street
And my white breath clouded the clear, sharp air.
Like brittle ice, our love had shattered
And I searched for its shards in vain.

240. Observations
PHYLLIS MARY FARLEY

I sit busy at my office desk
I look up to see the Winter sun
Shining coldly on the garden lawn.
I look up to see the Summer sun
Shining warmly on the leaves which
Hide the Summer garden lawn
And wonder where the time has gone.

241. Persephone
ADELE DAVID

Day swells as death seeps away.
The embryo sun caresses
her dark eyes as she rises,
waist deep, from within earth.

A butterfly emerges
out of her pupating heart,
poppies fall from hair
rich as the rhythms of the sea.

Taste of pomegranate seed
lies long forgotten on the lips.
The new moon fills –
this is Demeter's season.

Persephone longs for green blades,
for blossom become damask.
She waits for the fecund rains
to wash her live again.

242. dreaming of a hot summer day
AMANDA HEPTINSTALL

sun bleached sun drenched body
plunges deep into icy blue
emerging gasping salted molten drops

bodies stick to scorching plastic
buses wait in lines sighing
heat waves slowly rise

bitumen melts
bodies sweat
the cicadas call
sprinklers turn
mingling with the sounds of evening
beer tabs
ripping
in a sea across the suburbs.

243. August
PAT WINSLOW

This act of dropping seeds
and dusting them over with your feet
has its counterpart.
But it's more than reminiscence.
You raise the old roots
to see how deep they've grown
how wide they'll have to search
to find the new ones
and make their fierce embrace a home.

The measuring month –
how far to go
how far you've been.
August is like 60.

When I am august
I shall wear my traveller's joy
with silverweed and loosestrife
and peel away the old bark
to grow another ring.
I'll slip into myself
circle meeting circle
and be fat like ripening plums.
My weathering sun
will fix discovery forever
in the menopausal earth.

Yet I'll still be soft enough to burst
when the first punch
of clench-fisted November hits me.

Bury me then
but give me an august farewell –
no wasteland gestures
no starched words from men's black books
no flakes of hope.
Be warm. Be flesh.
Be real. Remember
It was the fall that I succumbed to
and not the winter's chill.

244. The Isle of Mull
PAMELA JAMES

I am content to sit today,
No urge to stride the rocky shore;
The sun is warm on Mull in May
And I can wish for nothing more
Except that words would come to mind,
An essense of this lovely scene
To hold against a wintry day;
A snapshot of Carsaig in May.

The burn runs bright, down to the sea;
A goose sits fast upon her nest;
White lambkins while their time away
And golden gorse is brave and gay;
On Mull in May.

Around my feet the speckled hens
Watch with expectant beady eye,
And cuckoos call across the bay,
So glad to be on Mull in May.

Beneath the awesome beetling cliffs
the gentle primrose covers all,
Drenched by the fast cascading spray
Of tumbling silver waterfall.

And when the sun has dropped from sight
Still will I gaze across the slope
Of lush green grass, where night by night
The Red deer file their stately way
to graze in peace on Carsaig bay.

But I must stop – I can't convey
All that there is on Mull in May.

245. Storm Cry: Elegy for Maz, 1987
OLGA ELIZABETH REID WILSON

After the Great Roar: the Silence.
Could this be the end?
But the sun shone on the snowdrops,
You watched me plant the year before.

I can not give these flowers to you,
Survivors of the storm and snow,
I can not cull them from their home,
To take them to your newest place.

So: I'll ask my friend to bring again,
More wild snowdrops,
Brave and beautiful in flower,
For your grave.

246. Coire Gabhail
LAURA WATSON

I came grieving to this grim, grey place.
Waters of a thousand ages seeped from the rock,
The tears of as many forgotten souls.

I would not have left you here amid the great drearness.
Yours was a happy spirit. Yet it was your wish.
Ashes strewn upon the granite of eternity.

And still I recall another day,
When sunlight led us to a hidden place.
A brave ascent to reach a cherished goal.

This glen where battles bravely fought and lost,
And man brought down by man in bleak despair
Can echo yet with songs of hope.

Mo Bràthair. You had your dream.
I will look for you on the mountain when October comes.
We shall walk a while, and I will remember.

247. Famine Graves
NELL SCULLY

no
shroud

nor
board

no
east—west
alignment

facing
the
rising
sun

no
mark

nor
prayer
inscribed

only
the
river

whispering
by

ever
lisping
lament
over
weeping
stones

(Graves of the Great Irish
Famine of the 1840s, at
Skibbereen, Co. Cork.)

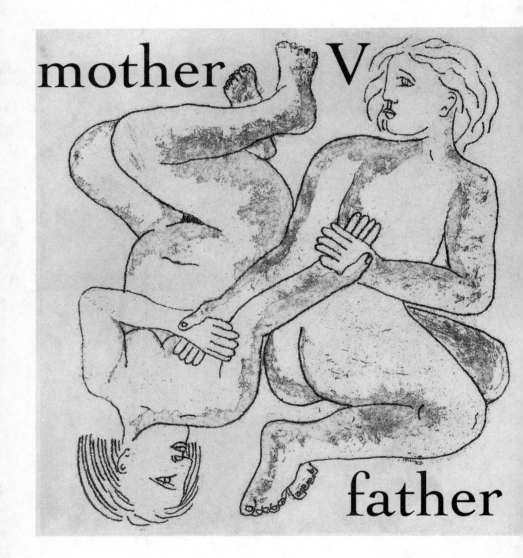

248. Don't Bury Me In The Garden
HARJIT KAUR KHAIRA

If I ever catch you, my aim will be to chop you
Into a thousand pieces
and bury you in the garden.

Realisation never signalled the significance of
my mother's words.
Her sense of pride and determination,
even when she talked about murder.
A lot of the passion is lost in translation.

People grow roses in their gardens,
People bury victims in gardens.
My mother wanted an exotic Indian Rose,
I could only act the part of a victim,
Let my mother's silver blade pierce
and cut the skin
as part of my penance.

I knew she would cut me in a determined way,
or skillfully slit my body in the way
she chopped vegetables for the evening meal.
I liked the way she cut aubergines
and fancied looking purple once the blood had dried
and I had to be buried in the garden.

Careful what you wear, careful how you paint,
so many shades of red, so many shades of blood.
My mother doesn't mention the red lips anymore,
but my relatives carry hoes and till the soil,
they're ready in anticipation
to place me in a plot
and bury me in the garden.

249. Power Dressing
DOROTHY KONIG

When I was young, my mother dressed me
In shades of yellow, pink and blue;
Clad me in the yolk–fed hue of chicks,
Trembling primrose, and jasmine's naked innocence.

By way of change, she bound me
In the blindborn pink of micelings,
The sweetie, weightless spin of candy-floss;
Wrapped me in a rosebud's layered fold.

She allowed the empty freedom of a cloudless sky,
The small wide–eyedness of forget–me–not;
A slight concession – duck–egg blue –
With teasing hints of things to come.

But green, she side–tracked for herself;
Drank in its depths from fern–lined wells,
Leaned against the height of ancient pines,
Breathed sunny hope upon its grassy hills.

She kept green for herself.

But now that she is dead,
And I stand motherless before my glass,
I see I suit green well enough.

250. Stolen Moments
SURJIT SIMPLAY

When I had the looks
They weren't allowed to look
When I had the drive
They weren't allowed to steer.
And now your time is running out
And mine is catching up
Do you wish you had let me be?

251. A New Star Galaxy
ANGELA HUNT

Though her head lies on a pillow of pearl satin
cold as the shadowless moon
the lips betray a wry smile.
In death she has left this dream
where we sift a thousand realities
to make sense of loss, the mystery reflected
in beautiful but silent turquoise eyes.
Until today, our clumsy invasion to divide
possessions divorced from memories
discarded in the dark mahogany drawers.

Plastic curlers, rouge and jewellery
trademarks of a life spent in service,
worthless without their stories.
Greetings cards, congealing creams in jars
are all unsympathetically binned.
Then the blue box that's dusted with talc
opens to a new star galaxy.
The special letter which would warm
a planet is wrapped in silk inside.

Faded and fragile from folding, it's
headed: The Central Fire Station
Jury Street, Wednesday 2a.m.
It begins "My Dear Jessie
I have been thinking of you a lot"
and ends with seven kisses,
"Keep smiling".
I scrutinise the looped y's
unlocking clues to his character,
meeting my father for the first time.

252. The X-Factor
POLLY BENNISON

She was loved as much as any,
Never lacked for material things.
Her life was full, her friends many,
But she never met her father.

She was clever, did well at school.
Took part in sport and games,
Never strayed too far, kept the rule,
But she never met her father.

She grew more pretty as years went by.
Had plenty of boyfriends, lovers too.
Ambitious, she set her aims high,
But she never met her father.

She married well, had children three.
Two boys, one girl, worth more than gold.
Life was good except you see,
She never met her father.

So in spite of all she wished for more.
A void to fill, an ache to ease.
Her life was never quite complete, for
She never met her father.

253. They Said He Was My Dad
MARY McDONAGH

They said he was my dad
And he looked so very sad
I thought "how can this be,
when you created me?"

But soon the answer came,
He had given me the blame,
For I was not as tasty
As a pint of good cool beer.

254. Daughter Lust
MICHELLE GRAHAM

When you were drunk old man, you
Marvelled through me
Passaging your lost daughter.

I do a dance for daddy, you
Press almond cakes in my hands
Plump them like the doughy hands of babies
Fondle my hair, call me your dog's name
Nuzzle me with damp kisses.

Nine whiskies later you would
Swell me into my actual age.
Your trick of bypassing adolescence
Clammy times when curves mount
Foul up a father's vision
Guilty mothers soak up blood
Imperviate daughters.

You caught me post fall
Contained
Container.

I am a father's fantasy
I am the son who shares liquor
Performs your Greek challenges
Barefooting spiked gates in a downpour.

Now I am the daughter
Breasty, bold,
You ripen me into a Rembrandt poise
License your roving all
Offer me up to be kissed by men.

Free drinks arrive
The fatted offspring
The philandering father
We play out a burlesque of wenches and cads.

Once you were drunk old man
I told you I loved women.

.../..

. . . DAUGHTER LUST

It besotted your fancy
You saw me leaking

You belched mutely
Scraped up a putrid language
Sucked up your kisses
Set your hands back upon your dog
Went daughter questing.

255. Beyond Therapy
FIONA CURNOW

I had the dream again last night
Where Dad comes back – well, not exactly back:
He says if I'm not gentle then he'll die again.
And through his words I hear that same,
God–awful groaning.

You nod and write 'Electra complex' in my notes
As if that wraps it up: you know so many words.
Well, I know words – I know
The place too many monsters play inside my head.

And I know things that you don't know: I know
That if you smile at monsters, they smile back.
And then you get to play with them.

<u>256. Isolation Ward</u>
ROSIE GARLAND

You're seventy,
propped up in the bed I crawled into as a child.
I reach for your hand and talk about my work
listening to survivors,
I still can't tell you yet
how people you called nephew and neighbour
did the same to me.
This way it's safe and so third-party.

But your gaze flicks away
and in that second I'm awake,
willing the air not to move
and snatch away the words
that slide from the side of your mouth,
framing your experience.

Your shoulders shrug
but your eyes give you away.
"It's the woman's fault" your voice says,
backed up by a lifetime's deafening chorus
of self-blame and isolation.

My passionate no
is tiny, feebly bouncing back unheard
from such a monstrous edifice of self-reproach.
I take a deep breath and look at the quilt
sending what love I can down my arm
and into your fingers.

We stand on the edge
of this old, stagnant pool.
How fair is it of me to stir the silt?

257. After Auschwitz (My Father's House)
IRENE BLACK

Usually
The door is shut.
It is an old door,
Salt–bitten, ravaged
By the steady chisel
Of the passing years.

Usually
It is firmly bolted
To keep intruders out,
And to fetter its sorrow behind
Bright veneers
Of fissured joviality.

Once
In the wine–heavy still
Of a summer evening,
When the laughter of good company
Hung upon jasmine–satiated air,
The door opened a little
Of its own accord.

And the rays of the setting sun
Teased a smile out of the terrible darkness
Within.

258. My Dad's Feet Went Scary
And Then He Broke In Half
HARJIT KAUR KHAIRA

Turbans scare people
strange hats and bandages
to be sculpted
cut or divide.
The hair was cut
the body revolted.
Psychosomatic, traumatic, phlegmatic, catatonic,
His hands and feet were at war.
Samson had it easy,
no turban had to be re–grown
only to find another host had taken over.
A parasitic country
that broke his spirit
in half.

259. Meeting of Currents
JULIE ROWELL

At Birsay Brough sand, currents meet in a race.
There was a time when this sight would heal.
Wild air and water charge at my head –
But father you will insist on stealing each place.
Your last look eclipses and yet nothing's revealed,
Only one fact is certain and that is you are dead.

A blue whale bone mounted on spikes,
Eagle–like, Dali–like, until you get close,
This vertebra, alive once, now atrophied.
But bones survive, throw shadows, cloak sight.
I came here to heal, breathe in the violet coast,
Hoping it could stem this continuous bleed.

Fishermen risked life here chancing the tide.
(You thought to drown, but said the sea was cold.)
Feelings collide, take hold, each thought's a lance.
(You chose a dog's lead to choke out the light.)
I came here to heal the wound, to be on my own.
But there's a meeting of currents at Birsay Brough sand.

260. A Good Man
JEAN BOWEN

She gave me the ten shilling note clipped to a sepia
Photograph. "Take this" she said "and have a mass said
For him. He was a good man."
Strange, I never thought of him like that.
He swept through life like a great wind howling
Carrying folk along like so much chaff,
Forcing them into corners
Making them do things they had never thought of,
Perhaps never wanted.
Yet though he caused havoc still he managed to create
Small pockets of calm and leave happiness in his wake.
When he spoke, people listened and remembered.
He was a Goliath. Huge. Great hands and feet.
Biceps thick as a girl's waist.
Stormy about cruelty, severe on wrongdoing
Gentle as he taught me my catechism
And soothed my childish fears.
Like a scirocco he blew me through
The troubled waters of adolescence
To the safe moorings of marriage and some other's care.
On the day he dressed in the bright whiteness of the
Hospital room
And heard them whispering behind the screens
He knew some greater force had entered his life
And he became a gentle breeze taking solace
In small things
Like planting parsley on Good Friday
And putting in winter greens he would never harvest,
Eating turbot instead of cod
And being even kinder to his wife.
He planned his funeral making me write
As mother fled crying from the room. There was a
Small tornado the day he made his last Communion.
While the smell of incense lingered in the room
And before the priest had closed his box,
He drank gin and smoked cigars – a last defiant stand.
I took the money and the picture from my great aunt.
He looked so young. I kept them both.
As a good man he was never worth ten shillings.
He was priceless.

261. Soft Shoe In The Automat
JEAN ALEXANDER

over blueberry pie
   he brings out
   clippings
creased & yellowed
   as his face

arthritic fingers
   unfold past days
   blurred images & reviews
   straw hat &
   2 tone shoes

by the light of the
   silvery doh-di-o-doh

he twirls a wicked cane
   in the neon glare
   tap-taps among the dog-ends
   on the floor

i applaud
   he sweeps a bow & then
   refolds his life &

   soft shoes

        out

           the

               door

262. Bubbles
JAN WOODHOUSE

(As a child, my mother was nicknamed
Bubbles, because of her resemblance
to the Millais painting)

in my dreams she is dancing
(i never saw her dance)

she is saying: I have to leave
people say it's silly at my age
but i have to
i say i understand

in my dreams
she is the woman
she never was

but in what passes for real

she is someone who
sits, smiles vaguely,
walks awkwardly

her memory dotted
with bubbles of forgetfulness

does *she* dream?
and do her dreams remember?

i remember
how she was always seeming
to want something better,
something different,
always restless, somehow

until the time came unnoticed when
she started to settle for less and

she swapped wanting
for comfort, little things

.../..

. . . BUBBLES

little things
that shrink
to the size of a smile,
a tear, what's the difference?

she nods
amused, amazed
at the very idea

263. Family
FOKKINA McDONNELL

I try not to lecture,
but she says I do.
She cannot make ends meet.
She spends too much money
on clothes
expensive food
and wine.

I tell her what to do.
She nods, gets bored
and walks away.
Her hair is too short
and her make-up
too bright
for her age.

I worry about her.
Going out at night
driving a small car
too fast.
And men.
She falls for their patter.
She likes the ones with good looks
who leave her.

I am my mother's eldest daughter
and she is sixty-eight.

264. Bathtime With Mother
JULIE WARD

We make the water
Rise up,
Threatens to flood,
Engulf the house,
With our gorgeous wallowing

I scrub her back
She washes my hair
We have always done this

There is unconscious beauty
In such voluptuous recline
She shares her ageing skin
With me, the first-born,
And I, three years post-natal,
Show proudly how my breasts
Still make milk

Long ago
I learned from her –
My body is a store of good things,
A treasure-house of pleasure
To nurture, annoint, caress

When no more steam rises and
Menfolk dance impatiently at the door
We clamber from our watery boudoir
And rub each other dry

265. Decay
JOY FRASER

"I never thought . . . " she always begins
as I help her from her nightly bath.
"Hush Ma" dropping a kiss on grey whisps
straying as her mind. Only eyes, velvet brown
a reminder of that other woman smelling of Chanel No.5
and mystery who cradled me to sleep another life ago.
Patting dry withered flesh we don't talk about the years
between; the war, the separation and the deaths –
too many now to count.
"Don't tell your father I can't wash myself"
eyes pleading complicity. "Of course not . . ."
(He's been dead these thirty years.)
Tucked – childlike – between sheets, pianist's
fingers playing a silent arpeggio up my arm
she drifts to sleep lulled by her secret music.
You've had a hard life Ma,
and now you've bequeathed it all to me.

266. Bathing
ROSALEEN CROGHAN

The skin on my mother's back and shoulders
retains its beauty,
her breasts are full now as ever,
and yet on the rest of her body some malicious worm
has gone to work
arranging her skin in folds like crepe paper.

Warm water and soap.

Holding on to my babies' fat slippery arms
my hand resting on the acceptable place
where the damp hair begins at the nape of the neck.
Washing them now together
getting slily at their ears
lifting them out to dry.

This is my strong and courageous time
when there are backs to wash.
Later I will sit on the side of the bath
for ever waiting for someone to come and help me out.
And these babies whose bodies I know so well
will discover mine,
bit by bit, wash by wash.
as I now discover my mother's.
Who once knew me so well,
she held everything about me
within the crepey folds of her skin.

267. Summer, Autumn
KARAN HEPPELL

I watch my Father regard the fells
in silence: his life gazes back
in the wail of the wind.

Fine traces of senescence,
so quietly restrained cut lonely
lines on his face, on the land.

Day after day, bleak criss-crossing
fields stir Autumn in his life.
I slide into the Summer of my own

with fearful certainty. I see myself
years from now so clearly in this man.
His world tentative and resolved,

revolves around wife, daughters,
grandchild. We nearly lost him
a year ago. Thick powerful hands

I thought could never fail,
let death crunch meanly over him.
Winter opened its doors, closed

them loosely in the next breath.
He discerns tomorrow only
as a better day. And as I watch

him looking out, I can see doors
opening on me a little more
each coming year.

268. Visiting My Mother . . . Aged Ninety
JEAN HAMPTON

'Come if you can'
The voice is sad. So I go.

At Brighton's front
Curled iron, rusted with salt,
Framed the channel.
Half memories leapt in fragments
Half hurting.

Under the pier lights, stark and spare,
I asked the man for cockles.
There were none.
'Everything's closing, Duck' he said
I drove on, past white chalk cliffs
That gleam in the last light.

We'd talked once of fairness,
Mother and I.
Rights for the workers,
Equality for women.
Today we talk of bowels,
Memory loss, and hearts that just wear out.

269. Losing Mother
JULIA PERREN

Divided by the train window
We spoke in signs.
You at last moved off
But nearly forgot
To look again and wave.
We laughed about that
Later on the phone.
I wasn't there at
Your final departure.
How dare you go
Without some signal,
Leaving me standing
On a platform alone.

270. Ceanothus
DOROTHY CRONIN

Ceanothus filled the world
With marian blue
While you went spirit walking,
Moving invisible,
Inviolate
Without our alien landscapes.

I touch the things you touched,
Move in the empty places
That you filled
And ceanothus blown
And rusty
Fills the space
That all my life was yours.

271. Cri de Coeur
HERMIONE RAVENSCROFT

Why don't you want to die, Mother?
You exhaust us with your whims:
Three times we've fixed the funeral
And chosen your favourite hymns.

"I don't want to be any trouble
To anyone" you said.
You're carried cold to hospital
Yet refuse to lie down dead.

We gather round your bedside,
Cancelling all our do's.
Then you amaze by sitting up
And asking for family news.

Your temperature was twenty–eight!
With tin–foil, flurry and fuss
You thawed and smiled and rose again –
But you'll be the death of us.

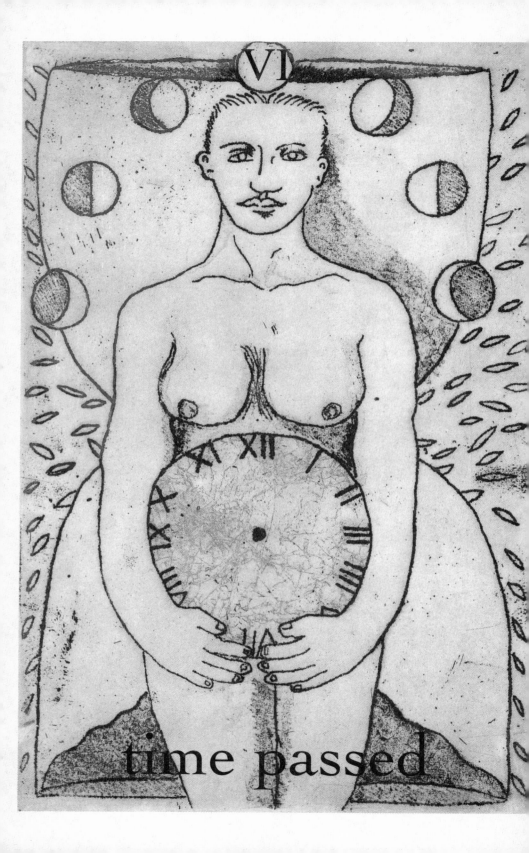

272. Red Herrings
JULIE CALLAN

I

Autumn invades the vale of Ennerdale.
Skeletal trees stand like herring-bone weeds.
Dogs echo messages back and forth. Recall the old days
– revert to wolf ways.
Motorists stop and stare at misplaced llamas
– far from the Andes.
There are sheep everywhere, everywhere . . .
And there is nothing, nothing to fear.

In places, it's "ANGLERS ONLY.
BY ORDER. NATIONAL TRUST".
We cuss, kick dust, turn car around.
Sun dazzles, yet fails to slice sugar-icing frost.
This scene is unreal. Not life as we know it.
Then a tornado streaks – intrudes.
I hold my breath . . .
Does this hi-tech power reassure?
Can't we go back to Nature – just a little more?

II

The "Lunar" computer reads:
'Your bones are fine. There's nothing wrong.
Sad to detect hypochondria in one so young.'
The nurse agrees, it could be the job I do – the stress.
'It could be a red herring.
I'm afraid that's the best we can do with these tests.'

III

You have stripped me down to bare bones
– unable to detect my danger zones.
I am left with a technicolour landscape – the Sea of Me.
Time to fear the future – to reflect.
So give me a life-line. Save me from the wreck.
Or wish-bone me a life of near-perfect bliss.

273. Catching A Crab
GILL FRANCES

High up in the wall is the window,
    a square of autumnal
    metallic blue.
The clean walls and untidy desk
    are friendlier:
They speak less of lethal rays,
    and lesions of the skin.

The doctor pronounces.

You hear a shot and, feeling no pain,
    look about you for a falling
    body.
Finally, finally, your eye meets itself:
    a small black pupil in your chest,
    a bloodless, insignificant
    pellet hole.

The word 'tumour' buffets your brain,
    and your resistant self
    (chosen from the several selves)
    rises to denounce
    the treacherous cells,
    the treacherous selves.

The awefulness, the awfulness,
    the terrible triviality
    of the wretched scene
    imprints upon your mind.

You are
    someone else's bad ten minutes
    before a coffee break,
You hold
    the winning raffle ticket
    when you wanted second prize,
You've been found out
    in a stupid lie,
Caught
    gossiping,

.../.

. . . CATCHING A CRAB

You've been locked
    in the lavatory, left
    shaking the door,
    absurd, ridiculous,
    undignified,
    not liking to call out.

Marathon failures,
Droppers out,
Losers,
Special cases,
Non-invitees,
And sufferers from halitosis
    instantly become siblings.

There is the fear of pain.

There is the question of conduct.
'The Etiquette of Dying'
    does not seem to be available
    at any good bookshop.

There is the silent acknowledgement
    of the signs.
You knew all the time that
    the match would be rained off,
    the trip cancelled,
    the treat postponed,
    the contract not signed.

Anger is present: it is
    a black hole in your chest,
    memories of night-lies,
    small-hours loneliness,
    small figures mirrored
    in the pupils of the eyes.
    It is cold, black water
    in the mind behind the eyes.

.../..

. . . CATCHING A CRAB

Cataphoric visions – white coats,
    medicines, masks,
    concerned serious faces of visitors
    bringing unwelcome reminders
    of ordinary lives, fortunate
    lives –
Blink past.

You press buttons on the keyboard
    of remembered thought,
    looking for a way
    for it to be "all right",
For your expectations
    to resettle themselves,
As a word processor
    rejustifies the lines
    to accommodate an alteration.

Control is bought
    at the price of despair.
Sealing off (the bunker from the torn world) . .
Abandoning (the fort to the savage hordes) . .
Throwing away (your baby to strangers) . .
Letting go (the fingerhold on the rock face) . .

You are in the present continuous
    tense closing down
    running away
    rejecting
    sliding

If you could hear the clock ticking
    in this digital age,
You would notice that barely thirty
    seconds have elapsed
    since the doctor
    finished speaking.

And the sky is still blue.

274. "A Light Gleams . . ."
BRENDA WALKER

It comes from the Latin
MIRACULUM
from MIRARE – to wonder at.

Just nine months and cell upon cell
the foetus grows
confident, unrelenting,
a gross lump
as clear as headlines on a placard:
TAKEOVER BID
NATURE IN CONTROL.

It's only three months
and cell has erupted into cell
out of control,
dividing, sub–dividing,
in rhythm with the heartbeat,
dividing, sub–dividing.

I glean his grey hair
from the plughole, the pillow,
the jacket, the chair,
from my nightdress,
from my fingers,
from my lips
and know that I will never
be able to retrieve
those soft strands
plaited deep
within the niches of my
cerebellum.
We wait for the miracle.

275. Breast Lump
RENÉE HIRSCHON

Tiny crab burrows down
          excavating pebbles
flicking sand
          the grit of tears
In fear that stalks
          on tidal strips

When joy is spent
          what is left?
A crabwise growth
          that shows me all

I'm not the owner of my fate
          Nor mistress of my house
A steward of the land
          a guardian or a tenant
I care for it and pass it on
I wait upon the Master

276. In Mammoriam
GERRY HOODLESS

My breasts and I
Have had a lot of fun.
So I really shouldn't cry
Now there's only one.

277. NHS Wig
TERESA MIDDLETON

The woman sailed in
with that automatic smile,
an Avon-lady look –
prim, powdered, so perfect.

By that time I was bald.
Hairbrush full of dead locks.
Moon-fat in extra-large pyjamas,
sitting quiet on the hospital bed.

She opened her baby-pink case –
four wigs to choose.
Long blonde; jet-black bob; long chestnut –
and mine – the dirty-fair one.

Still smiling, she plopped it on my head –
'Lovely, natural look, dear – so slimming.'
With a final grimace
She left within seconds.

I paced the ward – a masquerade
of trained nurses, smiling patients.
'It's fine. It suits you.' They lied
about my new style.

An animal – thin rat or squirrel –
scratching my scalp. I tolerated
the Crockett look until, hot-headed,
I threw the vermin out.

278. Internal
ALISON GUINANE

It might be a weather-chart or OS map,
speckled all over with a nasty rash,
as dizzy contours expand and retract,
or lurch drunkenly.
Zoomed into focus, they sway side to side.
Odd when you're asked to visualise
your own innards in black and white
on silent screen:
soft tissue, muscle and gut,
palpitating organs throbbing with blood –
line drawing in your Science book,
late night Horror movie.

The instrument that enters me
was warmed first in the palm.
Long, narrow and very hard,
it stops. "Expose that!" he barks,
and stabs his button victoriously.
"Fibroid there. Had a family?"

He gazes at the screen dispassionately,
casually roams my inside.
"Here's an infection you had as a child –
some of your kidney withered and died.
Has total recall, they say, your body."
I twist to see, at an angle of ninety.

He's from Glasgow, has hands like haggis,
emits (to relax me) a stream of stories.
Ultrasound's his job, all day he ploughs it.
I listen, legs apart, as women do.
"In my youth I was a blacksmith,
then a teacher, slamming desk lids
on their little you–know–whats." (I did)
My cervix looms on the VDU,
pouts and fulminates: Mick Jagger's lips.
Adrift at sea, it slides and tilts.
The probe nuzzles my ovaries,
candelabra–fallopian tubes.

.../..

. . . INTERNAL

"Egg in there, unfertilised."
Cells I never knew I had dance in megabytes,
down through the dark to where I lie,
dissected and displayed in files
marked *Confidential.* Forever forty-five,
faceless and unfertilised.
Watching the cursor, suddenly it seems
we perform in Virtual Reality,
me and this man. "Bowel's full. Haven't you been?"
Suddenly I'm four again:
my mother, business-like, interrogates.
I squirm and look away.

That's it. He swivels and, removing rod,
wipes it clean, covers me up, switches off.
Slightly soiled and dented inside,
clinically raped, bound, gagged,
I wonder if he's realised
how long since I was probed last,
and try to think of what's intact,
beyond the reach of ultrasound,
but – wheeled into the corridor –
remember only *Catch 22,*
a pilot's guts spilling out,
and the offal-carts of abattoirs.

279. My Friend The Dentist
FIONA ROWAN

Come in sit down quite comfy there
I'll just adjust the moving chair
How's the family open wide
Let's take a little look inside
Your husband's sick oh deary me
Cavity nurse upper left three
Shame about the cricket team
There really is no need to scream
It doesn't hurt these days you know
My youngest's learning how to row
What about the village green
Cavity upper right fifteen
Ulcerated right hand cheek
This front incisor's looking weak
What was that that you just grunted
You've joined a group against fox-hunting
Quite right too such needless pain
Let's prod that cavity again
Just as I feared you need a filling
Let's get on then with the drilling
You want a jab well deary me
No stamina now that's it you see
Relax don't jump it won't take long
Have you heard my nurse in song
A pleasant sound and so relaxing
Now please don't look like you're collapsing
Five minutes now for that to take
I've just preserved a four foot snake
Would you like to see it no
Just thought we'd pass the time you know
Now tell me if you feel an ache
And we'll just take a little break
Shame this drill's so old and worn
My sister's baby's just been born
Open wide head to the right
Sensation will be very slight
Well deary me what do I see
Another gaping cavity
Well never mind we'll do the lot
Weather's certainly getting hot

.../..

. . . MY FRIEND THE DENTIST

You're sweating dear so that must prove it
This dreadful mask I'll just remove it
Now to the job oh sorry chum
Still what's a small hole in the gum
Just pass the paste nurse one two three
No visitors I hope for tea
Scrape scratch spit oh lovely noise
How do you find the price of toys
Quite outrageous yes I see
I do so very much agree
A clamp on here my you do jerk
How's your boy enjoying work
Doing fine I thought so good
Just remember now no food
Finished now come back next week
There's four more in the other cheek.

280. Nurse's Song
CHRISTINE SAGAR

Can this be where we worked so hard last night?
I still can see the soles of shoes upturned,
Dead movement as the stretcher lurched through
Doors, or tilted up the dirty concrete steps.
The touch of love he called for never came,
Only the kiss of death had time for him,
Then frenzied hammering of our strong fists
Snapping a rib or two in three attempts
To start the heart that stalled so long ago.
This morning there are flowered curtains, sun,
Kids run or jump, clutch packs of crisps and smile,
Bored mothers glance through glossy magazines,
Complain about the charge for parking space
And say "This health service is crap" again.

281. Convalescence
RUTH PARTINGTON

One more seafront
To walk at a slow pace,
Passing soft tamarisk
But with no ecstasy,
My body like a wooden puppet
Hard to handle.
This nothingness of the sea landscape
Is what I welcome;
So much of the healthy world
Is wasted effort.
Did we learn to use our infant bodies
And forget the wonder
Until this ward–wound
Set us all back to nursery status
And drew together
Like a nightgowned family of girls
Women society decrees apart?
Why are we working now to get our strength
To tend our tiny households,
Fight for our petty selves
And guard useless possessions,
Forgetting this emptiness
We now enjoy?

282. Depression
SHEILA CHURCHILL

Thin pencil line of shallow breath,
not up, nor down,
but horizontal

No register on this flat plateau
of air–filled lungs,
and pumping heart

Just grey and numb,
and still and quiet,
a nothingness so monumental

283. Insect Body
BRIGHID SCHROER

Bony, white, fish-like, I sit curled in the bath
With one leg over the edge to keep the foot
Incisions dry under the bandage – post operation.

Under the tap, I curve like an insect rolled over,
Legs waving, pale underside creased –
A child's thin belly, long legs,
The water gushing warm over my shoulders,
The white enamel cold against my skin.

This is the body that wakes in the dark
Falling, when round the flapping of the heart
Nothing lies, nothing holds,
And my head may be wedged like a praying mantis.

284. Illness
ELIZABETH BIRCHALL

I didn't have to think about my feet;
I strode around and steered my limbs unconsciously
While my brain hammered out and beat
Ideas and actions into shape
With heedless energy.

But now all activity and energy is shrunk
Into a dim, dumb sense of a marionette drunk
And unstrung, bones fallen flat from every joint
All jumbled on the bed.
A rag doll crushed and torn, whose sawdust leaks
In little heaps from every point . . .
No will of mine can animate
These sticks and tattered rags
But others' hands took hold of me;
They cup their hands around my life
And cherish it and nourish it,
Hold me in trust till I am fit.

285. Anna
ROSY WILSON

When I reflect on
your hard work to stay alive
I cannot believe

you had to revisit
a dependant infancy,
struggle to survive,

use your strong will
to remain our Anna still,
in spite of great pain,

until you could laugh
with your friends and recover
sharing your courage

with all who love you
and your spring flowers
were replaced by summer roses.

286. I Just Want To . . .
NICKY JOHNSON

I just want to . . .

Work,
Go for a walk,
Run up and downstairs,
Pay taxes,
Run . . .

But those who want, don't always get.

287. Return Visit
MOLLY ALLEN

I brought you tea,
sat on your bed to talk
and start the crossword.
You said, 'Time goes quickly
in the mornings', and would not
let us linger.

I showed you Greenstead's wooden church,
its Saxon walls decayed a little now.
You were enchanted.
We talked, and drove through Essex villages
in soft October sun.
You helped me clear the shed.

One day I told you I lacked patience
with the old,
never thinking that meant you.
You were my friend.
Later you needed reassurance
and I was shamed.

288. No Dominion
(In Memory of Chris)
PAULA BURNETT

Cast up on a bone dry island,
nothing but sheets to knead into bread,
no sail on the horizon to return you home,
you endure your Galapagos, your hot rock bed.

The racing reel rattles. Darwin's film's unwound.
Crisp as a ginkgo leaf you stiffen, honed to bone,
a premature blizzard of days stinging your unblinking eyes.
Forty years gone at a spring: the great bound.

Suspended inert, old limbs shrink, twitch,
pupa skin thin as paper ash,
the message clear in magic negative
that this racked transformation's rich.

Yet, locked in your tower of pain
your skull's will's still a beacon
whose beam sweeps far and sharp as ever,
though more dark waters shoulder between.

289. Held Together
V.G. LEE

Guy Fawkes 1992,
Kilburn High Road standing still.
Between grid locked cars
weave Steve and Jim,
their smiles at twenty yards
infectious.
Cold knuckles touch,
broad shoulders brush
their ancient sheepskin jackets,
bought together, worn together.
"Fireworks", Steve shouts,
waving a carrier bag.
"Three rockets",
"One Catherine Wheel",
"No damp squibs".

Months slip by,
no word and then,
"I wish I had a gun",
Steve's face in mine,
his carrier bag tearing between us.
"Look here", he says,
"Me to BMA,
to doctor, solicitor – mine, his".
Paper currency spills across
the misted bonnet of a Volvo Estate.
"For god's sake, only pneumonia",
Slaps more letters down,
"And their replies?
Aids related, old man,
from we regret,
to none of your damn business,
skillfully hidden, evasion and lies.

"me to his family,
father, mother,
people I loved,
people I trusted,
sister, brother.
See here again, written by hand

.../..

. . . HELD TOGETHER

when I could hardly think;
three – four pages.
Them to me, a paragraph.
As we deem fit, right and proper,
best if I, meaning best for them,
keep quiet, forget, disappear."

Kilburn High Road, wet and filthy;
"Happy Christmas, bright new year",
I shout from twenty yards
to a convalescent who won't get well.
Misery infectious.
History suffocates
beneath life transcribed to ink on paper.
Held together
by dogclips, rubber bands,
green string tags and grey box files.
Belief suspended.

290. I Knew A Woman
ROSALIND GODDARD

I saw a woman dying before me.
She drank some wine,
smoked a little dope –
and her friends came round
to look on,
wreathed in health.
She was concerned on our behalf, about
what was left in the fridge –
as if those pale sausages were important.
She made it easy and we went along,
skitting like sparrows on a slippery edge,
picking up small snippets, and dropping them
half–digested.

She faced us,
and there we saw ourselves.
She beckoned us forward,
allowing us to grasp,
but we did not,
a little of how it feels.

We pulled our outdoor clothes close,
and that tender occasion
became a short act,
another afternoon out.

Eventually we left
kissing each other lightly on both cheeks
promising to come again,
hastening away –
to a safer place.

291. Seasons
RUTH PARKER

I had a friend who knew that she was dying
and on one autumn afternoon
arranged to have her summer clothes
all bundled up and sent to charity.
This action showed a stoicism
not attainable by me –
I'm sure I'd keep one sleeveless dress
reminding me of hot sun nearly scorching cotton,
one light–weight skirt
making me think of summer evenings drinking wine,
sitting on wooden benches still retaining heat,
one pair of sandals that my mind would scuff
through forests spicy with wild garlic flowers.
These clothes would be a signal that some hope might
still remain –
or if not, they could help me through the winter
of my dying.

Nevertheless, my friend was right –
she didn't even live to see the Spring.

292. A Poem of Remembrance
After Watching 'La Traviata'
VIVIENNE WACHENJE

So I buried my face in the follow of his
neck,
But he was still warm
Therefore, how could he be dead?

For, only some moments earlier,
Through his oxygen mask, quite calm,
"I love you", he'd said,

The rare, honest comfort of a weeping
doctor
As he laid his hand upon my arm
Gave me consciousness that life had ended,

Then I buried my face in the hollow of his
neck,
Yet he was still warm,
So how could he dare be dead?

293. Visiting
JOAN BULMER

She'd got it right this time
(he'd lost his pout)
he liked the playing cards she'd brought –
he laid them out

Red hearts and diamonds
he hated black –
(the spades and clubs
stayed lying in the pack)

The picture cards
her memories flooded back –
the King, the Queen, the Jack
the old, the young
in red and black

The Knave beside the Queen
(she had resisted him)
the King beside the Queen –
his face still looking grim

He'd been her King
and she his faithful Queen
the cards revealed the past –
what might have been . . .

He had forgotten her –
she tried hard not to feel
the anger and resentment deep inside;
her heart belonged to him
her love had never died . . .

She watched him deal
ate biscuits
drank her tea
and chatted to the nurse occasionally.

294. Lost For Words
GILL HORITZ

She praised oaks and beeches
season after season,
until a winter came
and 'trees' lost its sibilance,
fell into silence at the sight
of dark conifers beckoning
from the garden's edge.
Quick as a breath she found
'*those green swaying things*',
words flaring on the edge
of a tongue struck dumb.

Nouns are dying
yet still witterings rise up
of half-remembered sentences
eliding into their own sense.

This may be the last season:
I cradle her meaning,
fix it on paper, no longer fear.
Her minding's gone.
Without using the right words,
we take a panoply of turnings
in our giddy chat. And return
to the window again and again,
where blooms blossom,
which can no longer be said.

295. Sally, Nearly 90
ANNA TAYLOR

I carry with my left hand
Paint with my right
And can cut bread with neither

But still at it, I said.

No, I can't smell that rose, throaty-pinks though –
So much I could tell you I've lost: purses, keys
My waist – that sort of thing. Look at those leaves
Meshed fine as crystals
Sheer red; a silk-green pledge
This sunshine

Still at it, I said.

You know, my hat
My stick will outwalk me

Not almost 90, I said.

Pass the pastels, the matt paper –
I'd sooner have this little wood to
The cathedral –

How my old shoulder's aching,
Ha, sub specie, one of only two

Your hand's still not shaky
And, still at it, I said.

296. Age
LYNN THOUME

You're only as old as you feel she said
Well, that can vary a lot,
Depending on the time of the month
And how much money I've got!

297. Reflections
ELSPETH WALLINGTON

Looks are the barometer of the soul:
A weather-guide to the state within.
Life's emotions are reflected there.

Time was, I looked and saw reflected
Those emotions that I longed to see.

Time is, I look and see reflected
Only those emotions that diminish me.

298. I Looked In The Mirror
HEATHER JANE BUTLER

I looked in the mirror and saw my mother
Somewhere she had not ought to be.
For behind that full length, bevelled glass,
It really should be me.
Where had I gone? Had it been sudden or slow?
Would I be back? and how would I know?
That the elderly woman with such a familiar face,
Is not permanently here, myself to replace.

299. Release
CYNTHIA CAMPBELL

I lived alone and lorded it
Through my beguiling days.
No boss, no claims, no gentle words,
No carefully intended praise
To ease me down the tracks of care,
Of candles, glitter, festive days.
Confinement ended in release.
I lived in peace.

300. One Room Culture
JOSEPHINE McCORMICK

Redeeming one room culture
Promised youth freedom from mother
A room of ones own, a one room culture
Containing aspirations along with the furniture
Containing past and hopefully not future

At what point the rhythm broke
The self contained to containment a shift thats significant
The dream once of a home with a garden
A lover, a husband, a partner with commitment
Twenty five years for home with a garden
Thirty to fifty and then barren

You weren't wise in your madness,
Caught in one room culture
Indeed the promise came true
Freedom from being a mother
A room of ones own, a one room culture
Containing aspirations along with the furniture
Containing the past and the past repeated as future

301. You Say
LORRAINE CARTER

Sometimes I feel so
alone.
"Understandable", you say.
"Living alone."

But I feel so distant
even when I'm with others.
"Understandable", you say
"Can't trust lovers."

But I fear being all alone
Growing older and colder.
"Understandable", you say
"Don't we all?"

302. Iris Summer
NANCY LINDISFARNE

So I explained with dignity.
And oh, as long as three times three and more,
The dark-veined monster swished and played music
      at my thighs.
So I chose that elephant-eared, lizard-lidded truth,
And marvel at the spanking armfuls of irises
      when I sat by the gate, laughing.
And I try to hold onto each morning, the silvery
      shrub borders and those flower names.
I have never stopped wanting purples and golds,
      flecks of cinnamon and velvet.
And I still love to see hollyhocks when all else
      is slowing.
The excitement will be me, as if my body
      never idles, refuses to be serious.
And my legs and knees, they too refuse the
      thickness, the hard rough clay, and prance.
My feet, high-arched, celebrate the sky-blue
      scent of irises.
And I still remember petals which touch discreetly.
I covet those lustrous eyes kaleidoscoped in
      the myriad curls which make me lissom;
Made me dare to have my hairline punk-pierced
      and my ear-lobes graced by wire.
Remembering this, I am astonished when they say it's
      a pity, they are now faded, all salt, and in retreat.
I can look back. The summer cloves were meant as
      presents and had to be shared.
In my imagination I climb up the fence to the bolt
      and open the secret gate.
And I am stunned by the hot, hazy flick of
      that irreverent iris summer.

303. Replay
JAN PORTER

Players shift with Time,
rhythm of living.
Doors close.
Denizens depart
      to other people,
            other places.

Sleep-drifting,
we kaleidoscope the Past –
re-arrange the landscape,
embellish foolish edges,
erase the foolish smudges,
shade in the 'might have beens'.

As memory distorts –
sad, unwise infatuations renounced light years ago,
decant such bitter-sweet pot-pourri of desire –
we'd slither back,
yet have nowhere to go!

Beneath the private skin of lost lovers,
we surely surface, too;
thrindle meaningfully back like some old film,
ghost out of stowaway photo albums –

Someone they could have known better,
could have known.

304. Life's Like . . .
KATE GILLIE

Life's life taking a walk in the park
                      after dark
There's just one thing
you must be sure to do
Sneak up on all the monsters
before they sneak up on you

305. Swansong For The Womb
PAULINE PLUMMER

We are a row of women
without wombs;
silent, letting go.

The surgeons have stripped our
cavities and pouches,
have scraped and gutted their trout,
bled us clean, Kosher, Halal,
skimmed off our sins,
stitched up erotic dreams
inside our black wool.

We are gourds,
mangoes without stones,
a row of matrioskas.

All our seeds have been sown –
nothing stored against siege and famine;
if there are tares in the wheat
then we will eat each other
or hallucinate with hunger.

Once we were pomegranates,
with the callous patina of youth
popping with bitter seeds in sweet juice.
Now we are soft and white,
plump as late sloes,
our spittle tasting of wrack,
novices in a late vocation.

306. An Old Woman's Smile
CAROL HUGHES

As she slides past me the smile on an old woman's face
      hangs
      in
      the
      air
daring me to follow

The secret of a child who has just learned the skill of
hopping;
standing on her head.

The mirth of letting senses dart where they will

      wriggling
      out of
      the tight cocoon
      of do's
         and don'ts.

307. The Rembrandt Exhibition
SUSAN MAYER

Out of date women up from the country,
here for the Rembrandt with London to do.
Re-living the tube map, the rush of commuters,
the places we worked in, the men we once knew.

Out of date women, surprised at the tourists,
confused by the changes, relieved to arrive.
Cool in the National, peering on tiptoe,
finding each other like bees in a hive.

Out of date women watching our purses,
buying a postcard to show what we've seen.
Portraits of women, respectable housewives,
nothing remains of the girls we have been.

308. Bon Voyeur
JOAN PLANT

In the days of juiciness
the wineglass overflows,
Endless is the Vale of Years,
The hourglass on hold.

Dust of ages settles on
the ripe and hoary head.
Pinpointing the vintage, full
blown and gaseous.

309. Words of Wisdom
MANDY PRECIOUS

Wrapped in her rainbow wool bed jacket,
she thought she was invisible.
Lined up, a queue for words of wisdom,
her grandchildren, waiting patiently
for visiting time to finish.
She talked to her hands.

Why did they wait, these rows upon rows
of children – staring up as though
she might say something worth listening to?
She had no pearls of wisdom,
no great or final revelations –
only her baking to do,
only her raspberries going rotten
for the want of a strong back to pick 'em.
Only knitting she could no longer finish
and sewing she couldn't see.
She thought, profoundly,
"The difference Benny Hill has made to me."

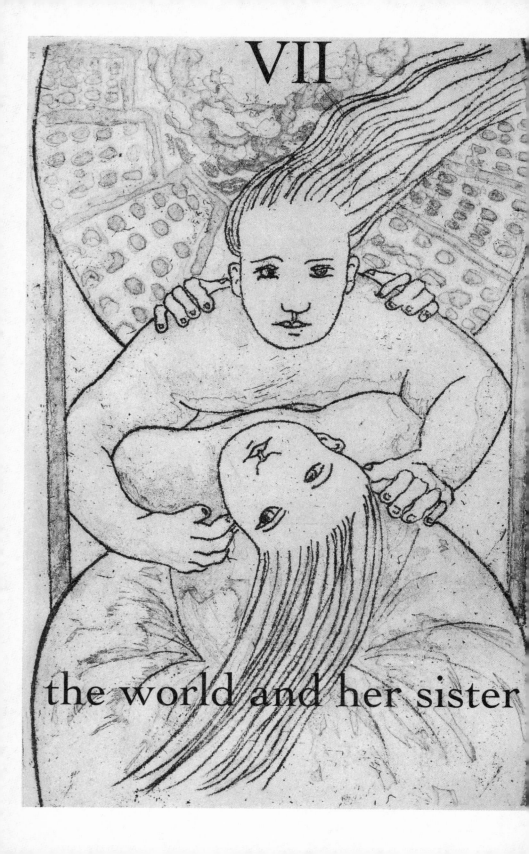

310. Quest
HAZEL RENNIE

Oh can you hear the song of the stars?
The rollicking voice of the Sun
The bugle call from the planet Mars
    And the chimes that reveal
    In their echoing peel
Why the rings around Saturn were spun?

They have blown down the light years to beckon you, friend,
    You will travel with us to explore
    On journeys to which there is never an end
Or a now and then or before.
We'll be free as a bubble of air in the sea
Or a shell in a desert of sand,
Free as aliens only are free,
With a freedom only we understand.

And if you can hear the rhythms of space,
The wild tumultuous reel
Of whirling orbits burning their trace
    And the throbbing hum
    Of the asteroid drum
In the turn of the Galaxy wheel,

Know you are destined with us to follow the quest
A true born daughter of Eve,
A desire for knowledge and, deep in your breast,
A belief there's somewhere a truth to believe.
We will hold while we can to threads that Eve span,
And the Web to her plan we will spin,
To the rhythm and scan of the Weave she began
We will turn and return to begin.

Then we'll dance with the stars to the Galaxy Song,
A reeling riotous fling!
And our echoes on Earth will be loud and long,
    And we'll keep the sound
    Going round and round
'Till Earth finds the True song to sing.

311. For Matthew
ELLEN ROSE BARTLETT

Dark in the eerie of the cat loud night
When rain and bluster thunder in the roof
And creepers fingernail uncurtained panes,
Sleet sweeps blisters gold against the light.
Though kitten-curled with children huddled tight
No bell nor book nor candle can be proof
Against sleek horrors lurching through the lanes
Slack jawed and staring, sockets blank and white,
Afreets and goblins, barrow wights and ghouls
In sere procession circling the green,
The unnamed dead, the unborn in their cauls,
Unknown and awful, waiting to be seen.
Unbar the windows, open wide the doors,
Embrace the dark and make the chaos yours.

312. The Beast
ALICE HARRISON

Touch this animal and it will
Stir from its slumber.

Caress it and it will
Rise and begin to slaver.

Leave it then and it will
Jerk away, tossing its head.

But ride it and its rhythm will
Move the earth.

313. Blue Angel
VIV HOWARD

Only she knows
What the future holds.
An orb in her hand reflects
truth and light,
a steel blue glance
in the frozen night
reveals all . . .
If only we were open to the signs
We would be caught
before the fall . . .

314. Before
SILVIA KUFNER

I write before I go to sleep
I smile before I leave
I love before I'm loved
I kiss before I go
I cry before it's over
I know why before I'm told
I care before I'm asked
I dare before the time
I know before
But I don't know why.

315. Lucid Spells
GUIA K. MONTI

I know
That saving oblivion
Will not lull my soul to sleep
And that draining visions
Of heaven and hell
Shall ever flicker
Through my besieged brain.

316. You Cannot Restrain
GUIA K. MONTI

You cannot restrain
You cannot oblige my soul
To stay out of this,
You cannot ask me not to feel
Or say there is
Too much feeling.
It is not up to me
To blend the grains of emotion and sanity.
Freedom is all I need
To vent my anguish
Onto the deaf ears
Of a quiet wind.

317. Pain
JANET FREEMAN

Your face screamed
Silent pain,
Wrecked spirit;
Quietly you spoke
Tales of rejection,
Early hate,
As the rain beat on the glass.

Enveloped in sadness,
You rouse yourself
To fearsome rage,
Imbecile frenzy
At life, the unfairness of things.

That anger
Was for another ear
Dead, gone, dissolved,
Unreachable.

You feel for your keys,
Smile, apologise, and are gone
To a world empty of comfort.

318. Jesus
GENEVIEVE YIP

Carpenter me a place
     for solitude
           and grace
Carpenter me a soul,
     just so I see it has no mould
Carpenter me a Jesus,
   not one that is carpentered but
  metamorphosed;
Carpenter me nothing else
     but hundreds and hundreds of
sea shells;
Carpenter me out of
           affectation,
Carpenter me into
          disintegration
Carpenter me
freedom,
So I am nothing else but flying wisdom

Carpenter me death
for I have seen enough
to want just a muddy grass wreath over
  my designated trough.

319. Lapsed Catholics Relaxing
ROSIE FAUPEL

Philadelphus
Decked out in delicate Bread of Hosts,
Wafer thin;
Bars our way in
To the late June garden.
Strings of pale morning light,
Finger a frail veil,
Worn for her first communion.
We, genuflecting, gently push her aside;
She, 'child bride', nodding a pardon,
Sprays fragrant chaliced dew
To annoint our laughing skin.

Lou's chaffing throw away line
Tossed with mocking throaty laugh;
Throws her own thin veil,
Cloaking half–
Spoken apology
For this untamed urban oasis.
"That'll teach you to come to Brummy,
Learn how the other half lives!"
Does she seek blame, catharsis?
Am I a priest, empowered to judge
Or bless?
I press past,
Playfully nudge
Her ribs.

320. She Said, He Said
CHERRIE WARWICK

She said:
"I would have been here sooner,
but I bound myself to watch the seasons in the faces
of my family and my friends.
Thinking I knew their need of me, I waited,
to urge their climb and on looking up,
fearful of the height,
would stand to break their fall
and then urge again.
Or lead restless thoughts through the formless maze
that is the mind,
nodding understanding.
But I grew tired, my time stood still in shadow
with jealous eye I looked away
and knew my heart would follow."

He said:
"Your journey is not over."

321. Life And Love
SYLVIA TYERS

What have I done that is so wrong
That I cannot forgive?
A kiss unkissed, a love unloved,
A life I cannot live.

What have I done that is so wrong
That you cannot forgive?
A task undone, a song unsung,
A life I will not live?

We watch the wars, the daily death,
The crime we cannot solve,
And watching powerless, absorb,
For we may not absolve.

What have we done? We crowd our days,
Create, and earn, and fret;
We smudge the memories of love,
Neglect them, and forget.

Our doom is, to grow old and stale
And charmless and obscene.
The mist of busyness comes down
To mildew what was green.

How can we help the children love,
Who shrug away our touch?
Will they refresh our sagging lives,
Which *seem* to hold so much?

What have we done that is so wrong
That they cannot forgive?
A kiss unkissed, a love unloved,
A life we do not live.

Give us the strength at last to find
A life that we can live;
The kisses kissed, the loving loved;
To comfort, and forgive.

322. Sweet Grapes
MARY HUBBLE

Why is it that defeat
Always seems to come
To the people who try
To be nice?

Being nice invites
The kick in the teeth,
The stab in the back,
The left in the lurch.

Winners take all,
And leave nothing
But the scent of victory
Behind. A mere whiff.

The smell of other people's
Victories is often
In my nostrils.
It sickens me.

Here am I, being nice,
Doing the right thing,
Missing out on all
The rewards of vice.

Sometimes I make the odd
Ploy, or plan a strategy,
But when it comes to battle,
I funk it and retreat.

Maybe the ones who win
Find the fruits sour,
But I suspect that
Their victorious grapes are sweet.

323. 30 Years On
HELEN POSKITT BINGHAM

It can take thirty years
To understand something
That'll change your life
Or to experience light dappling
Grey earth and leaves carving up a swaying sky.
But again, on Monday a hard crystal
Wedged in something you do
Can cause the inner landscape to turn its gaze other
And suddenly change its hue.

Aeons of ageing linear emotions
Line the woman in her sheer nylons
Wash over her trapped at her allotted space
Be it office, stove, or whilst staring at her face
Through the mirror as she quakes.
Subservient to the fortunate
Fatigued for eternity,
She, determined and pale
Stumbles the long corridors
Between creaking swing doors
Held smugly open by superior beings.

No light at the end of the tunnel
Look up to heaven between the buildings
As a way of escape.
Lose all boundaries,
Blend with the flakes
Of snow, melting on spikes.
A head on the rusty railings of life.

Corrosive linear anger and graphs of despair
All this, while hoovering the stair.

324. Plans
SUSAN WILSON

I've plans for this and plans for that
To buy a house or perhaps a flat
I write of this I write of that
A poem, a novel, a play to enact
I hope for this, I hope for that
My health restored; a world that's flat
I read of this I read of that
War and violence, greed and tat
I'd solve the problems of this and that
I'd find homes and jobs and charge no VAT
I've plans for all this and plans for all that
I would change the world at the drop of a hat.

325. Life In A Wooden Bowl
PENNY HARDMAN

1993 I bought a hoover – guaranteed
child/ren: Tom, 5
Leisure Card Expires
Way high on a mountain with my baby
and granny's garden.
The lino–cut made a card,
To dad with love.
Twice a student
once mature.
Over 600 simple phrases
for everyday situations
And a variety of dead batteries.

326. Steaming
JANET FREEMAN

The head of steam rises,
Gathers, promises
Strength, rebellion,
A new start,
Clarity, decision.

Steam falls, dissipates, clears,
Fearless visionary
Steps from the chill,
Humbled thoughts,
And sets the bath mat straight.

327. It's Only Natural
CARMEN WALTON

I tried it once, the natural life.
Yogurt, raisins and brown bread.
Then I got to breathing,
you know, the dust shifting,
lung busting grabs of air.
Then running, jogging and moving.
Lying in dark rooms to hear the sea
and imagine damp leaves under foot.
The truth, saying it like it is.
Truth, the nature of things.
But it wasn't natural.
I craved for plastic and the falseness
of shrink wrapped frankfurters.
I've been lying for years.
No one could handle my truths,
it was all too much for them.
I'm so out of touch with nature
that it's only natural I should return
to shallow breathing, shallow thinking
naturally sinking into a synthetic state.
Pleasure me with plastic until I feel fantastic.
Calm me, embalm me with something from a can.
Spice me up with some M.S.G.
It feels more natural, more like me.

328. The Mask
SHEILA SPOONER

She showed society a different face.
She laughed, she danced, she drank the wine.
A role played out for all of time.
But deep inside, in a secret place
She watched and waited for a different pace.
For when she viewed a crystal's drop.
She saw the likeness to herself.
Falling she knew not where, did not care.
For she lived her life, like a thief.
Always taking something not hers, not even wanted.

329. My Womanhood
CLAIRE MOONEY

Delighting in my womanhood
I watch the deepening lines
Make their way towards another age.

Delighting in my womanhood
Broken veins map a different course
Then start the chapter on a previous page.

Delighting in my womanhood
The voice takes a lower tone
And mouths unspoken rage.

Delighting in my womanhood
I brush away the tears
And take smiling centre stage.

330. Bubbles And Troubles
ANGELA LORD

Do you remember
The games we played
Blowing bubbles through straws
In our sweet lemonade?
Then we grew up
And we both got laid
And we met and regretted
Mistakes we had made.
But you're not the same
As you were before.
There's a binful of bottles
Outside your door
You've a family to keep
And the bills don't get paid
And you can't drown your troubles
In sweet lemonade.

331. Pizza
KATE GILLIE

When eating pizza in public
always be sure to wear a plastic raincoat
That way you stay clean and dry and later
you get to lick the raincoat clean

332. Custody Tart
SUE THORNTON

Decorative display
Of lusciousness.
Poise, glamour
Midst clamour
Of telephone rings,
Raised voices, food.
Delicious delicacy
Wickedly wanton.
Tempting little piece,
Custardy tart.

333. Breadcrusts
DEBORAH SCOTT

Breadcrusts float on toilet water,
The unattractive betrayal,
Of misery and guilt.

Leaving behind,
My only positive thought.
That whatever I eat,
Avoid bread.

Because the crusts do not sink,
And the bowl will need to be flushed twice.

334. For Anyone Who Ever Had A Bosom, With Sympathy.
SARAH CARPENTER

When I look in the mirror,
I see an ample bust
And I wonder, if it is wasn't there,
Would I really be that fussed?
I think I might enjoy it
If all people had flat chests;
The bliss when blokes no longer stood
Conversing with my breasts.
Some say I should be thankful,
That I am so well endowed;
They say,
". . . if mine were half the
size, I think I'd be quite proud".
But they don't have the hassle
Of just lugging them around:
They don't have old pervs querying,
"How many to the pound?"
They don't have trouble finding
A top that nicely fits,
They don't mumble to shop-workers,
"The problem is my tits".
It's a bit silly moaning though, really;
After all, they're a big part of me,
I expect they're much better than silicone ones;
They won't explode and I got them for free.

335. Breast Behaviour
JOAN MAIZELS

I'm a big breasted woman
who needs support
for appearances sake
cupped rounded
firmly clasped uplifted steady
no wobble no bounce.

I like it best when set free
slack languid we prepare
for sleep, they drooping
drifting as I stir
shapes soft indistinct
follow close and comfort me.

336. Cycle
TISH OAKWOOD

Woman she bleeds,
and the world that is turning
feeds off
and burns up
her seed.

Without her sacrificial flow
driving the mill wheel
of the world
all life
would clot.

337. Pandora
FAY MARSHALL

Eve eyes a fruit that's fixed just out of reach;
A trail of blood starts snaking through her days;
One careless act brings on a final breach,
Innocence lost, sour taste of the world's ways.
    Curious, vexed at knowledge incomplete,
Eve's bold descendant slowly lifts her hand . . .
She never sees the red stain on the sheet,
A swarm released, a pregnancy unplanned.
    A threshold crossed, a door no longer closed,
Pandora, tricked, abashed, hangs down her head.
Shrill voices buzz; a pause; a question posed;
Arms empty; circling curses; growing dread.
    Full cycle now, with membranes ruptured, torn,
She cries in joy; and a new life is born.

*(In classic mythology, Pandora raised the lid of a
forbidden box , and released a swarm of curses;
but she also released hope.)*

338. Only Once
ANNE BORN

Clouds swim through the sky at the short day's end
salmongrey from the northwest
to spawn rain over the east.
Trees raise their branches, talk back at gusts.
Waaargh! I hear them in my hotbed of dreams
mixed with the sea's gasps. The rain's cycle,
months', years', circle our life as the woman's
who walked this path after similar rain,
boots clogged, sacking–backed, wondering
if her mother still lived or if she would see
her lie like the fallen trunk she has to climb over
as she has climbed over so much and only once
seen sun and moon rise at the same time.
As salmon and clouds too swim through the world once.

339. Duet In The Malvern Hills
NAWAL GADALLA

We walk as British women
sturdy and unconcerning
sensible and sure
hearty and ruthless
polite and yet . .
rage a scream
let it mourn
the stifled cries
the daggers drawn
the passions dead with limbs of lead.
I am hot, I am buried alive and
I am lost in your formality
that demands of me that I am a
British Woman.
I am not. I am Arab, I am silk,
I am heat I am heart.
I have freedom in my step that
will not be controlled.
You cannot bury me alive.
Reckon with me and notice,
my British Woman, what I have for you.
Notice where it hides
and when it lies
(betrayal by approval and form)
impacted on the shore.
swim swim fly escape
usurp
the marbled stones that keep you cold
oh British Women.

340. Outsiders
HARDIP SHOKAR

Outsiders to your pain set the rules for your life,
first somebody's daughter, then sister, then wife.
        Always a fighter,
        but never the winner.
        Never forgiven,
        though never the sinner.
        Can't stand the distance
        of familiar faces.
        Can't stand the nearness
        of unknown places.
        How do I do it?
        How do I get there?
        Why am I going?
        Do I even know where?
        Now where?

341. A Foreign Woman
MARIA BUJAŃSKA

She changed the map's colours.
Different towns grew on her skin.
A different river rocked her to sleep.
The rains had a different taste, spring a different smell.
An alien flag fluttered in her hand. She spat out the old
        language, had new words made to order.
She turned the tap of a different history,
        grew old in an alien forest.
She dreamt at night of the motherland, beckoning her.
She grew wild. The streets mocked her,
        people eyed her with suspicion.
She planted a lime tree, shook off alien words,
        bathed herself in thyme,
burnt the flag. Returned to the town she was born in.
Familiar fields blossomed on her skin again, ants began
talking to her in Polish.

The poems above and below were translated
from Polish by Barbara Plebanek

342. Legacy
MARiA BUjAŃSKA

I inherited a horse from my grandfather,
the white star on its forehead.
I inherited a mug from my grandfather,
cut-glass.
I inherited Hunger's portrait from my grandfather.
He went hungry, made hats, and he darned life's holes.

I inherited tact from my grandmother.
(I never lean out beyond the rhythm of the ticking
metronome.)
I inherited an iceberg's calm,
the face of the surprised Moon.
I learned about the circus of the world from her,
the jump through fire,
through an iron hoop
in search of truth.

From my father I inherited the pain of being.
I took the sharp smell of life from him.

As a legacy from my mother I got good nature,
the Sun in a wire crate.
I got a window frame
through which I look into space,
a ladder to climb
and a warm blanket against the winter's snow.
A crayon – to draw goodness,
a slow march through the day.

I didn't get freedom as a present,
I didn't get a blue bird.

I was handed poppy seed thick with choice,
a question mark
and the future's red cypher.

343. Heredity
GWYNETH HUGHES

my mother was a mermaid
who left me on a beach
because she was ashamed
of my long legs and feet

I walked to the first village
they said I'd be their queen
because my skin was speckled
because my hair was green

draped in an ermine cape
wearing a jewelled crown
I called to the rolling waves
and threw my sceptre down

my mother from the ocean
rose with a school of fish
and paused, her arms flung open
to blow me a mermaid kiss

howling I must be powerful
before diving under the surf
back with two-legged people
I ignored her imperial words

and married a fisherman
instead to make him king
then bore eleven children
five with tails and fins

into the welcoming waters
I tossed my infants home
they burned me as a heretic
a witch, to charcoaled bone

a layer of fine ashes
covers the land and sea
my offspring will hereafter
breathe and swallow me

344. Beyond Bounds
CATHERINE JEFFREY

As the wood crackles
so does her skin;
as plumes of smoke drift
they carry her dust;
as the onlookers leave
her soul takes flight –
no-one breaks the spell
of the healer, the licker
of communal wounds,
for the air will cradle
her legacy of wisdom
till the next witch rises
to inhale her charms.

345. Maelstrom
TRISHA JONES

River mud clogging
wet-dark hair,
she rises fighting,
churning water.

Gagged, her mouth
works violently,
hopeless screams:
unheard.

Silent now, the crowd
await the verdict;
a child sobs quietly,
tearless.

Limbs straining,
she sinks again;
body shimmers,
unshaped.

Innocent.

346. Woman In Black
KAREN HAYES

Woman in black with your black
shades on and your fat white leg
breaking free through the slit
of your long black dress

and the fisherfolk plunge
in the bellies of the eels
and the blood oozes out
like the fat white thighs

of the woman in black
oozing out of her skirt
in the thick black night
like the souls of the fish

from their slit scaled bowels
breaking free in the blood
of the fishermen's hands.
And the woman in black

sits alone on the pier
with her thigh swinging down
and her soul swinging free.

347. On William Strang's Painting 'The Cafe Bar', 1915
PATRICIA TYRRELL

The men – blank, ordinary, Homburg hats
or bowlers, ties of navy/white,
discreet moustache or glasses or a beard
wispily trimmed like some old weary ram's;
dark overcoats, city-pale cheeks.
There's nothing here for us.
Whereas their wives . . .

Pre-votes, pre-independence, yet one woman holds
a patterned cup as if she'd weighed it
exactly, weighed her man too; her heavy eyelids
mock at the painter and refuse him entry,
her full lips smile, her hair (massively falling)
is forest to stay lost in.
We need such women.

Behind, escorted by moustache-and-pincenez,
another cranes her neck in red-blonde curls, ignoring.
We have seen this curve a thousand times
in our young children, lost when they grow older.
She cranes and shrivels him (her wide hat perched
absurd, a plunge of turquoise roses).
She's all our infants.

My mother too, in ragged photographs
between her nineteen-thirties chores, showed just this tilt
of scornful head. Past apron, kitchen door
and me her gaping child burst her uncaged
bold stance, her travelling stare, with heavy lids
ready to fall and shield
those private journeys.

Shall we in turn, next century,
(stared at in photos by our grandchildren) retain
the fiery aura, the assurance
of secret destinies beyond the picture
branding the future like an open O?
We who've achieved so much
shall we be memorable?

348. Pianoforte Supreme
ROSE McKENZIE

On Monday, after Easter Day,
I played a friend's piano,
But someone else's fingers
Seemed to ripple on the keys.
A talent, liberated by wine
And by good company,
Sang, that afternoon, of beauty;
And my imagination soared.

349. Ooh, The Power!
VALERIE LOUDON

It isn't quite a racing bike,
There are no lights or gears,
The basket on the front is bent,
The seat's known many rears.
It needs a fit contortionist
To ring the blooming bell.
I climb aboard and sit erect
And peddle away like hell.
My little woolly hat is jammed
On tight about my ears.
I put on speed, my skirt rides up,
My petticoat appears.
I catch a thrill when flying over
Traffic-calming bumps.
They're not so good for cycle springs
But not so bad for rumps.
I never mind the aches and pains,
Ignore the shaky knees,
The uphill ride against the wind,
The tendency to wheeze.
'Cos I am Green and I am Free
As downward now I wheel.
I'm cycling round my neighbourhood
And ooh! the power I feel!

350. Waylaid
CARO LEE

Loving you somehow
I became waylaid
Immersed in other people's washing
Enclosed in over heated kitchens
My arms elbow deep in potato peel
For french fries I could never eat.

My life became submerged in
Washing dishes, dusting doorknobs.
(You've heard all this before.)
School runs and swimming trips
With other parents' spotty kids.

Not guilty, I now buy packs
of frozen chips and magic treats at M&S:
Tender green and orange vegetables already peeled.

Distressed one dark dank afternoon
I went to the Library to shelter from the rain.
By accident or yet a miracle
I was reborn somewhere between
Bronte and Virginia Woolf.
Oh yes! Oh yes! I cried.

Slowly, silently it came to me
A memory of future visions of hopes and dreams,
And I remembered, I thought we were in this together.
Loving you somehow
I became waylaid.

351. Slut Dust
SARAH INGRAM SHAW

Bet you'd never have guessed,
Couldn't even imagine
all the desires I've hidden under the sofa.
Ha! You thought it was dust.
Slut dust you call it.
No. It's time better spent.
There on the draining board
Ha! You thought it was dirty plates
Lazy cow you call it.
No. It's time better spent.
And over there on the shelf by the telly
You thought it was untidy papers.
No. It's all my time better spent.
And I won't sweep them under the carpet.
I'll nail them to the front door to ward off discontent.

352. Ironing Board
SARAH INGRAM SHAW

Second time around
and he still hasn't learned
I'm ironing board.
Go to work creased what do I care.
Or else, Be Bold, Be Brave
Be Ironing John.
New man
Come out of the kitchen cupboard.
Oh, and while you're ironing
Be a love and do a couple of shirts for me.

353. Preparations
CHRISTINE CURRY

I washed up all the dishes,
lying in the sink,
I wiped away the layers of dust
and I gave the plants a drink

I picked up all the debris,
lying on the bedroom floor
I straightened all the covers
Hung their coats behind the door

I made sure all was orderly
with no more disarray
and then I put my coat on
and then . . . I went away.

354. The Knitting Pattern Family
CAROLYN BROOKES

They sold you warmth they sold you wool
They cost just one and three
They stood in chunky Arran
The pattern family

Cast on knit two increase to four
Stitch up your secret soul
A mother sweatered life away
To spin her family pure

Mosaics move fashions change
I wanted to be free
One slip, cast off, now I'm trapped in
The unpicked family.

355. Epilogue
CARMEN WALTON

Can't squeeze into your space
or wear your face
then disappear without trace.
I'm going to hit first base,
pioneer my own race
finish packing my case
leave this place.

356. Final Cut
ANNIE BLUE

someone said   this is what
you do   and she did it
someone said   this is what
you are   and she was it
someone said   this is what
i want you to be   she
became it

and there lie the shining
red scissors   blades apart
glinting and gleaming
slowly she began to
snip around her body
cutting herself out of
their picture   until all
that was left as she slipped
away   was her outline
around a gaping grey
hole   and nobody
noticed the difference
no one even knew that
she had gone   no one ever
realised that somewhere
else   there was someone else
carefully cut out with
sharp red scissors

357. The Punctual Man's Bereavement
PATRICIA SWANTON

"The funeral's at ten-thirty,"
he tells her coffin,
striving to keep her within
the discipline of time.

And now she'll be confined
by days and months for ever –
birthday and wedding day,
the day she died, and
the day she was buried.

There'll be comfort for him
in her captivity;
he'll visit the cemetery
every week and sit
among ancient trees, his
heart sad, but at rest.

The watch on his wrist
ticks, quietly
marking the bounds of sanity.
Each day he gets up at seven,
eight at weekends.

But the anarchy of decay
smoulders below ground.
There's no monitoring
the slow fox-trot of time.

He will not know exactly when
her face falls away,
or her kneecaps drop.
Check his watch as he may,
she'll do this
in her own good time.

358. Society
KATRINA PLUMB

They'll want you if you're witty,
respect you if you're rich,
parade you if you're pretty
and then call you a bitch.
Behind you.

They'll cheer if you have children,
they'll leer if you cannot,
they'll jeer if you have problems
they fear might be forgot.
Remind you.

They'll leave you if you're lonely,
bereave you if you're broke,
retrieve you if you want some peace
and chide you if you choke.
They're vicious.

They'll love you if you laugh a lot,
they'll shove you if you're scared,
above you when you're in the pits
they'd duck you if they dared.
Malicious.

Detest you if you drink too much,
despise you if you don't,
depend on you if you've got dough,
defend your life they won't.
Abuse you.

A tower of strength – society,
with power to shape your view,
pathetic in the piety
with which they purchase you
And use you.

359. Underneath The Arches
ALLISON FAIRMAN

Stainless steel's shiny gleam
tired mothers, children scream
mop and clean, milk shake falls
run around to the manager's calls

50 quarterpounders, can't I go home?
Not for hours, polish more chrome
ajax sanitise, face you can see
no grease no mess, no pickles go free

hustle hustle, win the fast food race
never ending profit chase
hassle pressure, standards to meet
must keep smiling, no aching feet

suggestive sell, push donuts and pies
large coke is that sir? another bag of fries?
service quickly, can't have a queue
sixty seconds, next person through

shut the doors, eleven o'clock
crew still here, more floors to mop
pruned fingers from washing, no-one has fun
taxi driver, some time past one

day off at last; called in for a shift
sun was out; black cloud won't lift
waiting at home, work in one hour
wait a bit longer, rush for the shower

another day, same thing again
top up the coffee of drunken old men
frying the food, hands do not burn
watching the clock, hands do not turn

leaving at Christmas, staying till May
want a new job, always the way
papers are empty, future looks bleak
leaving tomorrow? maybe next week.

360. The Woman Outside The Warren
LOU FRANCES

What do we make of her –
The woman outside the warren?

Ah, she's lonely,
She's anti-social.
But she's no-one to care for,
Well who would want her?
She looks so worried,
She looks full of scorn.
Must be hard to pay the rent,
She'll scrounge it off the state.
Her heart must have been broken,
Her type don't have them to break.
Her man might be in the forces,
She'll be a man-hating feminist, for God's sake
She's living in the middle of nowhere,
Good, that's where she can stay.
There must have been some tragedy,
So, we'll let grief keep her away.
Maybe her children got adopted,
A better life with someone else.
A teenage pregnancy, I don't doubt it,
Aye, just to ensure her a house.
We don't see her at church on Sunday,
Her sins will keep her at bay.
Maybe she'd join the WI, not the PTA?
Invitations aren't called for, if she wants, she'll say.

361. Suburban Monsters
MENA DIGINGS

Monsters coiled behind closed curtains
Tails twitching and twisting the nets,
Noses and eyes pressed to the panes
Encompassing the neighbourhood in the bile of their breath
The blinkered, opaque outlook on the world beyond.
Curtains crinkle imperceptibly.
Scouring for imperfections, indiscretions.
Reptilian tongues tattling, rattling on and on . . .
Reporting, distorting.
Waiting, wondering.
Knowing all, yet understanding nothing . . .

362. The White Cat
RUTH STERN

Only the magpies show themselves
In my street
And the white cat of course
Doors shut
Windows closed
Heavily shrouded in net
The milkman who I never see
Leaves bottles of milk
Quietly
Outside closed doors
Later I look
And the bottles are gone
But I saw no one
Except the magpies
And the white cat of course

363. Lying To A Market Researcher
MARION BODDY-EVANS

Eighteen to twenty five.
Married. Very happily.
Two. First a boy then a girl.
Detached. Four bedrooms.
Buying.
Professional.
Over forty thousand.
Two. A Range Rover and a BMW.
Three. Lounge, kitchen, bedroom.
One. In the bedroom.
Waitrose, Marks and Sparks.
Paul Smith or Armani.
Fifteen to twenty.
Thirty to thirty-five.
Hatchards on Piccadilly.
Three times a year.
The Caribbean, Thailand,
and two days at the Edinburgh Festival.
No, I never enter competitions.

364. Truant
ANN WHITEHEAD

Gary Green was always good
And went to school, as children should.

On Monday morning, they hit him hard
With a baseball bat, in the school yard.
His mother said, 'You've cut your lip!'
Gary said 'It was just a slip.
I caught my toe on the kerb.'

On Tuesday night, he was going home
When they demanded his watch 'on loan'.
His father said, 'You careless bloke!'
Gary said, 'The strap just broke.
I'll look for it tomorrow.'

On Wednesday morning, they had a knife
His only thought was to run for his life.
His teacher said, 'You're late for class.'
Gary said, 'The bus went past.
It left me behind. I'm sorry.'

On Thursday night, with cigarettes,
They burnt his hands and then his legs.
His mother said, 'What have you done?'
Gary said, 'It was just some fun
With fireworks. I was stupid.'

On Friday morning, they found a hose
Soaked him, and then poured paint on his clothes
The headmaster said, 'What's going on?'
Gary said 'There's nothing wrong.
I just got splashed by this lorry.'

Now Gary Green is not so good,
Doesn't go to school as children should –
He hanged himself last week.

365. Migraine
DILYS WOOD

This could be the biggest
Crime statistic of our time –
One murdered child, aged two.

The police call for witnesses –
Bear witness! Bear witness!
We all can. One society. One crime.
A finger of an English oak of evil
Splits into two young criminals.

"Supply a little of the jig-saw",
Police ask –
"From fragments of individual observation
We shall make a whole."
That's a good simile!
Shrugs, winks, non-observancies, backsliding, turning-
blind-eyes, easy-ways-out, letting-off-hooks, non-
punitive, nonchalant, distracted attitudes,
Led to these lads
Cracking up a child
Like an egg.

This crime affects us like a migraine.
Bloodred jackanapes dance before us.
Common scenes dazzle with supervening
Evil. Sick and in pain, we now see straight!

The generations' slowly loosing grasp
On the basic meaning of "Citizen"
Dumps the oppressive weight
Of jungle law on the youngest.

You know the boys, of course?
(Excuse me, this is classless)
Seen them around the shops?
God forbid, they live at your house!
Even today's youngest child
(As young as the victim)
Scuffles, pushes, head-butts, abuses, yowls,
Dolled up in bloated clothes,   .../..

. . . MIGRAINE

Eyes weary-ringed with hours of TV,
Tempers of snarling dogs.
On their second, third, 'fathers' some of them –
Or fathered by no-one they know.

"We have much to fear for our children",
That they should become murderers.

366. Back Pedalling
For Hans Christian Anderson
MAUREEN MACNAUGHTAN

What's the time Mr Wolf?
When we played last
Every street-door obliged.
There were few distractions,
Now the children catch
A giant tinder-box.
Jack never journeyed here,
This land honours the sphinx
Averted faces and privacy.
Seasons come with instructions
All is Bluebeard technology.

Once upon a long night
An enchanter took retirement
Since that shoemaker vanished
Few can charm the beast.
Let the Ice Queen rule
Through a desert of antenna.
Make the beggar woman
Offer a distant quest
And a dapple grey,
Restore that sense of wonder
If only for a day.

367. Mad Bureaucrat's Song
(With apologies to Lewis Carroll)
HELEN CLARE

I thought I was a liberal
    Attending freedom's call,
I looked again and found I was
    A brick within a wall.
"I have to keep the rules" I said,
    "I have no choice at all."

I thought I was for people's rights
    No matter what or who,
I looked again and found I did
    Not truly value you.
"You see, it's not my fault" I said,
    "It's what I'm told to do."

I thought I did my duty
    From within my given role,
I looked again and found I was
    A man without a soul.
"I weep and pray for you" I said
    "But it's out of my control."

368. Farming Poverty
KATHERINE M. CLARRICOATES

Green flat brown
this peaceful earth
grows humanitarians
by the crop,
careering
in others' poverty
drinking
weak tea
with academic alcoholics
eminent but anonymous
intellectualising
tentacled hand-outs
whilst passing
cucumber sandwiches
without crusts.

The poor snarl
at thin pleaders
thinking
they prefer to drink
cointreau
by the bathful.
Officials
spill the ink
on biting regulations
kicking pity
in slippered feet.
And god's
suspicious creditors
and all other fat bleeders
doing
for the community
whatever comes
naturally.

369. Ownership
SHELAGH BARTLEY

My round
Your turn
The form.

My programme
Your choice
Our tune.

My cold
Your worry
The misery.

My day
Your time
The patience.

My example
Your thought
Our lesson.

My feelings
Your temper
The problem.

Their problem
Our feelings.

Their patience
Our gratitude.

Their luck
Our envy

My land
Your Highness
The people
Their country
Our life.

370. Feeble Choices
DONNA PICKRELL

Washed up land of feeble choices.
Some have hands and some have voices.
Does it matter which you choose?
Some have luck, but most just lose.

Someone's name in flashing neon
Draws a crowd who pay to see 'em.
If I put my name in lights
Would I, too, whet your appetites?

Get a complex, see a shrink,
Or use it as a ruse to drink
Whilst trying to be a millionaire
By filling in the questionnaire.

Jump from rut and into furrow,
Looks the same but sounds more highbrow.
Still, you get a little kick
From thinking that you had the pick.

Someone wrote the moral guideline,
Placed me firmly in the sideline.
Here we play it by the rules.
Are we the good? Or just the fools?

I've been moulded by the system,
Shaped by someone else's wisdom.
Washed up here with feeble choices.
Some raise hands, but few have voices.

371. Harvest Home
GWENDA OWEN

Your place is empty this year.
You have gone
with a convoy to Bosnia.
Your intention surprised.
We mumbled support, contributed.
Paused to watch
civic farewells on TV.

Two days later
we dress the church for harvest.

Flowers flame walls;
apple mountains shine;
Pears by smug bananas squat;
grapefruits, lemons,
glow lamp–like near the lectern.
Fiery–scaled pineapples
explode in shoots of green.

We step back, consider;
Slice a melon in two.
Its red raw flesh, dripping juice,
enhances the display.

Above heaped vegetables,
the harvest loaf holds pride of place.
Sabbath done,
we'll break, with careless fingers,
into its glossy crispness;
find it too stale;
give some to Emma, for her pony,
some to Daniel, he loves feeding ducks.

Trucks rumble through darkness,
their crated ingathering
snatched
by frantic hands.

Your place is empty.
You'll miss the feast this year.

372. Dinner Time
EIRENE GRAY

I can eat chilli con carne
As children die or, watch
While prams and handcarts
Cross in Europe.

I drink a rouge at sunset
While cities burn and
Living skeletons
Suck earth.

I see
The futility of half of humanity
In the frame in authentic colour
With dinner.

373. No Choice
GILL WIDDOWS

Young women dance their ballet in a barren compound
Enclosed by stark barbed wires and guard towers.
Inside, sweet children, shelved and wrapped in sacking
Sleep unknowing.
Waiting to be removed and crushed
By men treading the pulp as it oozes from the great press
Blood flowing like wine, the harvest of disconnection from
Pain.
Release means to reconnect with hurt and suffering.
We have no choice.

374. Celebration: A New Friend
CHRIS HACKETT

I like the fact that you're fifty-something
and at my party you drank what some would call
too much.

I like your solid, no-fucking-about truthfulness.
The fact that your socialism is rooted
in stories so precious to you
and still you tell them and still you know
they have the power to burn, and that they must.

I like it when you go away for a weekend and,
coming back, report it as if it were
a trip to heaven. Because it was.

You colour my dream that it's possible
to be over-forty, or fifty, or ninety and still
to be in a state of wonder; and outraged
by all the new and old and endlessly repeated -isms;
and aware of the horror behind all
the seen-it-all-before news pictures;
and furiously conscious of the patriarchal
back-drop, front-drop, every bloody drop
we're supposed to behave ourselves in;
sharp as knives to the hypocrisy that says
we've arrived - in some Post-Feminist, Post-Socialist,
Past-Caring new age. And still to proclaim
the snatches of heaven as well as to fight like hell,
and still to be girlish and frivolous-round-the-edges,
and I think you are and I think I am
and god knows there's few of us enough about.

And so on a day
when all the flags I've waved at people
and all the flags they've waved back,
for months, are hung out to dry
and the wind blows hollow through me
and says how brave but small my efforts are
and the sun says: Is this all you've got to show for it?
I say: No, there's this one.

                              .../..

. . . CELEBRATION: A NEW FRIEND

See! how deeply coloured, how brightly edged,
how hard it's waved through its years.
See how it's been to Greenham and back,
how keenly it blows, how softly it wraps.
See how it catches the light!

375. And in the beginning . . .
NADINE VOKINS

men have named
the world, and so
have claimed
the world.
over time they've tamed
the world
now know they've maimed
the world.

women can blame
the men
and name
the men
who have maimed
them too
and shamed
them through.

the claim
is palpable
the shame
is culpable
but
is it possible
to quite reframe
the game –
to share a mutual aim?

and is it probable?

376. Collage Poem
Londoners eavesdropped
CLARE FEARNLEY

No thing can please me today

Cancer last time, shingles next time
it'll only be a cold next time

I've been drunk since Thursday

And I am what I still like to call a communist

They can snort if they want
and I don't mind them mainlining in front of me,
but I wish they wouldn't smoke

She's got a picture of a boy in her eyes
that she likes

377. A Bit Of Decorum, If You Please
MARIAN BETTS

A well brought up parrot, called Kelly,
Got addicted to watching the telly.
Until his owner, not amused,
Heard some foul language he used;
Now, after nine, he's read poems,
        by Pam Ayres, Kipling or Shelley.

378. The Role Of Mr Animus
In Producing A Poem
CORA GREENHILL

When it first comes out
a blurt scrawled on the page
all gangly like a new wet calf
all wobbly
I'm not intrigued at all
I turn the page
can't be doing with it
would orphan the weakling
feel no connection
certainly no commitment
to training and feeding
– it needs so much of me
to survive.

What we need then
is a good farmer to arrive
a tough rough gentle
husbandman.
He'll use his big spade hands
to turn my disinterested
heavy head
towards the trembling waif,
make me see it, sniff it.
He'll give me a bit of encouragement
say my name
fuss me a bit.

Finally, I may lick it
taste it
and with a tingling rush in the udder
own it.

379. Inspiration
JOAN FINNIS

You have a talent she said
Sit in my garden and write
About life love injustice
Irony and about women with cats . . .

I sat in her garden in the sunlight
My typewriter on my knee,
Hands crossed behind my head
I watched her mow the lawn instead.

380. Writer's Block
PATRICIA SWANTON

I wanted to write a mansion of a novel,
Edwardian or Georgian, with high ceilings,
and moulded cornices, elegant and spacious,
with a plot that ranged like a country estate.

Or a sturdy terrace of short stories
heft from mill-stone grit and blunt integrity,
reflecting the different thoughts
of different people on common themes.

I wanted to write a prize-winning article,
a deconstruction of post-modernist form
that would set everyone talking
as they walked past it in the street.

But I came right up against brick walls,
met locked doors for which I had no key,
and found myself in cultural cul-de-sacs.

And all I have now is a self-contained poem
with its own front door and a small gas-fire.

381. Philosophy
JOAN GALWEY

Poems tend to fly into my mind and woo it
When I'm driving against the clock, and no pen pat,
   Recalling the couple who could only do it
In a third class carriage, and in a tunnel at that.

My plight happens daily. I remember barely
Even the aptest unrecorded word.
   But how much worse was theirs, when you think how
                                    rarely
The situation occurred.

382. Playing With Poetry Is
MAGGIE NORTON

totally self indulgent.
The cerebral equivalent of
masturbation.
Orgasms sputter
one after the other
fizz and delight.
Only difference is
poetry offers
a lap of honour
for a roar of
public approval.

383. Footwork
(for Kit Liversidge, poet)
LAURAINE PALMERI

A chiropodist? All those years
tending feet, your head
bent over bunions, corns
and ingrowing toe-nails,
clipping and cropping the never-ending
growth of horn, while the quick
of the mind sprouted words
which ran to the ends of lines
like happy children descending
irregular steps.

You carved, shaped, trimmed,
filed, nailed down meaning
on the page.

384. Words
SHIRLEY RODDHAM

Words are thoughts released
Presented on soft pink tongues
Licked and tasted
To be offered as a gift.

Listen to my words
Wrap them in answers
Love comes from whispers
To become a pregnant thought.

385. Two
MARCELLA CULLEN

For every word I write
I lose two
Special
Secret words
No-one else can understand

Our lingua
Foreign pride
Stigma sounds
Pulsing in my right hand
Not yet formed

Saliva words
Wasted
On my tongue
I must not let too much go
I must not let emotions flow
But you already know
I might bleed to death

For every word I write
I lose two
One for my soul
And one for you
But you already know
I might bleed to death

386. Stories
JUDI BULL

I wrote you into my story
and you wrote me into yours
but the you that I put in my story
wasn't the you that you put in yours
and the me that you put in your story
wasn't the me that I put in mine.

When I find the me that I am
and you know the you that you are
maybe together we'll write
a different story and maybe
we won't.

387. The Stolen Song
VENETIA CARSE

Come back to my heart, my Song.
   He asked my Song to sing;
      I trusted him.
He took my Song to sing;
   he changed the Words, the Pulse,
      the Melody;
         he made my Song his own.
Can you wonder my trust is gone?

Come back, my Song, to my heart.
   You took my Song to feed
      your Ambition,
You deceived me with my honeyed words
   and I promised.
You took my hand, gloating:
   'Mine, now, and on your Death, still mine:'
You taunted me –
   and I wept.
For my Song had been the Wind's
   Breath of my Soul, not for Gain,
      but to distil
         the Air of Arcady.

388. Modernism? Post Modernism? Or Has Time Stood Still?
SALLY CLINE

Playwright intellectual,
Theme pseudosexual,
Play ineffectual,
Praise perpetual.
Doesn't it upsetual?

Art abstracted,
Public distracted,
Critics attracted,
Paintings contracted.
Is our judgment refracted?

Child sophisticated,
God antiquated,
Religion outdated,
Atheism, buddhism, taoism, overrated.
Whose fault if we are fated?

Girl brainless,
Man shameless,
Birth painless,
Child nameless.
Are we blameless?

389. Off The Wall
KATHERINE GALLAGHER

Rembrandt's Wife, no less steady than usual
is venturing a gavotte; a Munch Madame,
surprised by laughter, surprises her friends
with an intractable guffaw. Now, a Modigliani
Girl is bringing the house down –
she swears she is just being herself.

Tiens! Titian's Venus breaks her spell,
gets off the couch unaided
while a Lautrec dancer kicks off,
into the ceiling – such flair and more.
Raphael's Madonna slopes in,
sharp-eyed as her child. It appears
Renoir's Lady *is* bored with her
toilette; a Rubens Mistress has
turned the tables and is painting
old Piers Paul himself. A Picasso Femme,
about to leave, has drawn Pablo on the door
as a divided self. Meanwhile, Vermeer's Milkmaid
declares she is done with domesticity
just as an Ernst Nymph, dancing
out of the woods, invades the salons.

Let the party begin . . .

390. Cast Off
JANE ANDERSON

Sex shapes Dame Hepworth's
Posthumous sculpture garden
In her salty St Ives home
A shed left in mid–creation
Marble baubles, chisels and stones
She cast her bronzed offspring
As the casts of light flank the sand
As the fishing fleets cast their nets
As the casts of race pound the land
As the sea conceives its bays
Hewing out the womb
Yield, yield and yield
It's the foolish artist who delays
The cast off

391. On Hearing Nyman's Icarus Suite
KAYE LEE

Icarus dreamt it,
attempted it –
man's first flight.
Went too far.
The hot sun
drowned him

Breughel pulled him back,
suspended him
above catastrophe,
unnoticed in the business
of a rural day.

Auden observed this,
philosophised, paralleled,
remarked the ordinary
blindness to tragedy.

Icarus, failed, lives on.
Could success have been sweeter?

392. Malatya
JEAN FERNEE

Talking to the carpet seller
In Malatya
We concluded sadly
I would not buy the kilim,
Nor the brown yellow
Tobacco dyed, silk knotted
Carpet from the Black Sea coast.
The kismet was not right
Between us.
I could appreciate the subtlety
Of thread and colour.
I could read the subtext;
The eyes and fingers of women
And children sweated.
But instead we talked
Of Heathcliff and Catherine Earnshaw
And Emily Bronte.

393. Valediction to Walt Whitman
WENDY HOLT

Exit, Walt, old buddy,
Inept in a tight-lipped era
All that pulsating emotion, the torrent of words:
Forget it.

Life must be trampled down, the rude
Sore edge of feeling, hot with meaning,
Snuffed out in a tick, spitting tallow:
We haven't time.

We will wallow no more in the lull of rich cadence
Soft-hazy with sentiment.
Our backs to the wheel
We heave our load uphill
Till we crack.

And the mouths of children, crazy for kisses,
Are stopped up with sweets;
Dead eyes of husbandmen
Stare out at hopes' blight,
Heart's dear-bought truth
Turned off, cut down, shut up.

Today no music soothes:
We take pain neat.

394. Whether To Even Try
CHRIS HACKETT

Reading about a poet (man),
Whose early work, he says, was all
Linguistic elegance. Form. Scan.
And then he thought:
"Eh up! There's something missing."

Being a woman who likes to think
she's all Content, pith, heart,
with an ear that sings it tender;
and that this comes, in part,
from the quicksilver muscle that shimmers through
the survival-history of our gender,
(a deeply unfashionable view):
I'm at a loss to know what to do.
Or what took him so long . . .

Like knitting a jumper
with absolutely no
middle
but then again
who wears poetry?

*Editor's Note: Yes, we know about the split
infinitive in the title. The author points out
that, given the dilemmas women face,
"infinitives are among the least dangerous
things one could choose to, as it were, split".
Readers may judge whether the rest of this
volume has borne this out.*

395. Tailpiece:
A Tale Of Two Mice
VIRGINIA DIGNAM

Whenever I cried, as a child
my father would tell me the tale
of the two mice who fell
into a pail of milk.
One mouse cried piteously
and swallowed so much milk
it drowned instantly.
The other mouse struck out
courageously
and went around and around
the pail all night
until in the morning
it found itself
safe and sound
on top of a
mound of butter.

INDEX

Key to Symbols

AGE: a=Under 30   b=30–50   c=50–70   d=70+
WRITING POETRY:
A=Always   B=For Some Time   C=Recently
PUBLISHED:
@=Never   *=Locally/Own collection/National mag./Anthol.
LIVING: City or Country (Co)

305. Pauline Plummer, b-B-*-City

303. Jan Porter, b-A-*-City

323. Helen Poskitt Bingham, b-C-*-City

71. Laura Potts, b-C-@-City

309. Mandy Precious, a-A-*-City

202. Diane Pritchatt, b-A-@-City

208. Lesley Quayle, b-C-*-Co

271. Hermione Ravenscroft, c-A-@-Co

245. Olga Reid, c-B-@-Co

221. 310. Hazel Rennie, c-A-@-Co

111. Doreen Reynolds, c-C-*-Co

79. Wendy Richmond

132. Gina Riley, c-B-*-City

37. Lydia Robb, c-B-*-Co

57. Lucy Robeson, a-B-@-City

384. Shirley Roddham, c-B-@-Co

159. Marisha Rose, b-A-*-Co

228. Greta Ross, c-A-@-Co

182. Virginia Rounding, b-B-*-City

45, 279. Gillian Rowan, c-C-*-Co

279. Fiona Rowan

259. Julie Rowell, c-C-@-Co

210. Lisa Rudall Wortham, a-B-@-City

136. Anne Ryland, b-C-@-City

100. 280. Christine Sagar, c-A-@-Co

9, 183. Sally St. Clair, b-B-*-City

230. Lesley Saunders, b-B-*-City

65, 78. Kate Scarratt, b-C-@-Co

165, 283. Brighid Schroer

188, 333. Deborah Scott, a-A-*-City

247. Nell Scully, c-B-@-City

351, 352. Sarah Ingram Shaw, a-*-City

87. Helen Shay, b-C-*-City

340. Hardip Shokar, a-B-*-City

91. Penelope Sidney

250. Surjit Simplay

128. Sheila E. Smith, b-C-*-Co

59. Sheila Smith, c-A-*-City

328. Sheila Spooner

362. Ruth Stern

223. Barbara Stewart, c-C-@-Co

40. Greta Stoddart, a-A-@-City

85. Alison Stokes, a-B-@-City

89, 222. Ruth Stott, b-A-@-City

218. Glen Summers, b-A-*-Co

357, 380. Patricia Swanton, b-A-*-Co

140. Diana Syder

195, 229. Jane Tarlo, b-A-*-City

219. Mary Taylor, b-B-*-City

295. Anna Taylor, c-A-*-City

102. Pat Tempest

332. Sue Thornton, b-C-*-City

296. Lynn Thoume, b-C-*-Co

77. Lesley Towner, b-B-@-City

231. Jill Truman, c-A-*-City

321. Sylvia Tyers, c-A-*-Co

347. Patricia Tyrrell, c-A-*-Co

375. Nadine Vokins, c-A-*-City

232, 292. Vivienne Wachenje, b-B-*-Co

49. Anna Walker, a-A-*-City

19. Phyllis Walker, c-B-*-Co

274. Brenda Walker, c-B-*-City

297. Elspeth Wallington, c-A-*-Co

327, 355. Carmen Walton, b-B-*-City

264. Julie Ward, b-A-*-Co

320. Cherrie Warwick

127. Rachel Watson, a-B-@-City

246. Laura Watson, c-B-@-Co

108. Vanessa Watts, a-B-@-Co

237. Jan Whalen

163. Ann Whalley, c-B-*-Co

364. Ann Whitehead, c-C-@-City

215. Sarah Whitehead, b-B-@-Co

373. Gill Widdows, b-C-@-City

324. Susan Wilson, c-C-*-Co

34, 285. Rosy Wilson, c-C-*-City

243. Pat Winslow

32. River Wolton, b-B-*-City

365. Dilys Wood, c-C-*-City

181. Mary Wood, c-C-@-Co

262. Jan Woodhouse, b-A-*-Co

27, 28, 36. Joan Woods

177. Heather Woolley, a-B-*-Co

109. Pauline Wright

66. Joan Wyatt, c-*-City

81, 318. Genevieve Yip

104. Sally Young

233. Eleanor Zonik, d-A-*-Co